MW00932183

Faith:
In Your Own
Handwriting

Steve Davis

Copyright © 2015 Stephen Craig Davis
All rights reserved.

ISBN-10: 1519570120
ISBN-13: 978-1519570123

All rights reserved. No part of this publication may be reproduced, stored in a retrieval system, or transmitted in any form by any means, electronic, mechanical, photocopy, recording, or otherwise, without the prior permission of the author, except as provided for by USA copyright law.

Unless otherwise indicated, Scripture quotations are from THE HOLY BIBLE, NEW INTERNATIONAL VERSION®, NIV® Copyright © 1973, 1978, 1984, 2011 by Biblica, Inc.™ Used by permission. All rights reserved worldwide.

Scripture references marked NLT are from *Holy Bible : New Living Translation,* copyright © 1996, 2004. Used by permission of Tyndale House Publishers, Inc., Carol Stream, IL 60189. All rights reserved.

Scripture references marked ESV are from ESV® Bible (The Holy Bible, English Standard Version®), copyright © 2001 by Crossway Bibles, a publishing ministry of Good News Publishers. Used by permission. All rights reserved.

The "NIV" and "New International Version" trademarks are registered in the United States Patent and Trademark Office by International Bible Society. Use of either trademark requires the permission of International Bible Society.

All emphases in Scripture quotations have been added by the author.

All websites accessed 2015.

Cover Design: Glenn Davis

DEDICATION

To my amazing daughters, Nikki, Sierra, and Dominique. I am so proud of the women you are, and the people you are becoming.

Also, to my nieces and nephews, Alyssa, Jeremy, Rachel, Beverly, Kent, Kohl, Kirk, Kane, Brooke, Caleb, Joshua, Ethan, Sydney, Josiah, Dominic, Karis, and Malachi. You are big reasons why this book exists.

CONTENTS

INTRODUCTION

Imagine if everything you've ever learned was placed in three-ring binders.

All you know about math, history, the Internet, video games, the stock market. Everything.

In binders stacked all around the room, each one labeled with the subject matter. Some volumes thick and heavy from years of study; some thin, just a few lessons learned through failure.

As you look around, you see a folder labeled "Faith." You pull it out from its stack and open it.

Sure enough, it's your faith journey, whatever it has looked like so far.

For some of you, it is Bible stories you learned in Sunday School. For others it's blogs about the harmful effects of religion on society. Legalistic codes or free-flowing emotionalism. Racist rants or pleas to bring justice to the oppressed. Whatever has had the greatest impact on your view of faith, it's all there.

But then you notice something: Almost none of it is in your own handwriting.

Some is in your mom's careful script, some in your dad's chicken scratch. Some might be in your pastor's or youth leader's or priest's neat hand. The idea that religion breeds ignorance is in the handwriting of a television talking head or popular blogger or author. The paragraph exhorting you to love your neighbor is in the shaky scrawl of your grandmother.

A few brief, indecisive passages are in your own handwriting, but the overwhelming majority is penned by others.

Here's the thing: This is normal.

Most of us absorb our faith from the people around us. As we reach our late teens and early twenties, we often find that the view of faith we possess isn't really our own. It's the one given to us by others—or the one we built reacting against the views of others. And if we never stop to truly examine things for ourselves, that inherited view of faith is the one that we carry throughout our lives.

But whether you consider yourself a person of faith or not, if you are reading this book, I'm going to assume that at least a part of you is drawn to the concept of faith. And whether you are hoping to find a reason to accept faith, a guide to increase your faith, or a final push toward a permanent rejection, the thing you should desire most is for the final conclusions to be your own. You don't want your faith—or lack thereof—to be something you inherited from others.

Whether the decision is pro or con, you want the answer to be in your own handwriting.

That's one of the primary purposes of this book. To honestly examine faith, specifically, the Christian faith I claim; to strip this faith down to its essence, and see what it really means to be a Christian; to see if it makes sense at a logical and emotional level. And if you come to believe that it does, to give you the tools to write your personal faith in your own handwriting.

The first section of the book will look at the logical, historical, and emotional basis for faith. It's not an exhaustive (or exhausting) argument for Christianity. Books that focus on that area of faith fall into the category of apologetics and can be highly valuable. But in this book we're only going to (hopefully) show that Christianity makes sense, and that it also does a pretty good job making sense of the world around us.

In the second section we'll be looking at the faith itself, the beliefs that make up what some would call Historical Christianity. We will see that a lot of the beliefs you may find offensive about Christian faith aren't integral to the faith, but are actually just the way some people have personalized their own faith (or adopted and adapted the faith of others). Don't worry, there is still plenty of offensive stuff in Christianity,[1] but there's not nearly as much as you may have heard. Again, this section will not be exhaustive or exhausting. People who dig deeply into this type of material are called theologians and their books are called theologies. But I believe it will be comprehensive enough for us to move to the final section, the one we've been building toward all along.

In that third section, we'll talk personalization. How to take the basics of the faith, add in what we learn about faith both on our own and in community, identify our God-given passions, and fuse it all into a faith that each of us can call our own. A faith we can live with, and ideally, a faith that can give us a reason to live.

---

[1] The idea that we're all sinners, for instance.

Part 1:
The Foundation
Of Faith

1 DIRT IN TRANSITION

What am I?

That's the first question.

And in the broadest scheme of things, there are only two possible answers. While few would use this phrase, the first answer, the one many people give, boils down to, "I am dirt in transition."

Seriously.

See, everything on earth starts as dirt (or stardust, if you want to get cosmological). Somehow, some dirt developed/evolved into something else, something that had a quality we call "life." An ability to be self-sustaining and to reproduce. As they reproduced, some of these living clumps of dirt became more and more complex, from amoebas to sponges to fish to hippos.

Somewhere along the line, some of the clumps developed an amazing quality: self-awareness. They became conscious of their own existence. They wrote songs about it, painted paintings, created movies where they demonstrated clearly that they knew they existed. Glorified dirt created the *Mona Lisa*, *Casablanca*, and *The Simpsons*.

Then they died. All of them.

Okay, some are still alive and kicking (and making more Simpsons episodes), but the bottom line is that every one of these self-aware clumps will eventually die and go back to being, yep, dirt.

So, one potential answer to the question, "What am I?" is that I am simply dirt in transition. I am a clump of dirt that somehow mysteriously acquired the trait of self-awareness, then I maybe wrote poetry and maybe played sports and maybe even reproduced. And when all of the activity and awareness is over, I will return to being just plain dirt, useful as plant food or to fill an urn to be placed on a mantle by other self-aware clumps of dirt in transition.

If you're like me, that answer isn't very satisfying on either an emotional or an intellectual level. Emotionally, because for some reason I want my life to have meaning. Intellectually, because how a clump of dirt could acquire that desire for meaning is beyond this clump's mental capacity.

Which brings us to the second question, "What about God?" Because, if the answer to the "What about God?" question is "There isn't one," then the only answer to the "What am I?" question is "I am merely dirt in transition. Nothing about me has real value, and nothing I do has purpose."

So I guess maybe we should address that question, "What about God?" Before we look at the second possible answer to the question, "What am I?"

What about God?

Okay, if we want to be specific, the "What about God?" question is potentially three questions. First, does God exist? Second, what kind of God is He/it? And finally, how does that impact me?

Obviously, if the answer to the first question is No, God doesn't exist, then the other two become irrelevant, and we just have to learn to live with being dirt in transition. Which I don't like. But just because I don't like it doesn't mean it's the wrong answer. I don't like that Bill Belichick is the best coach in the NFL, but he still is. I don't like that if I bury money in my back yard it won't multiply overnight either, but my retirement strategy doesn't include magical money pits.

So, does God exist? I don't think there is any way to tangibly prove His existence,[2] but there are a number of things in the universe that point to it or hint at it. We've already mentioned one of those pointers, the fact

---

[2] Or else we wouldn't need faith, and Hebrews teaches that without faith it's impossible to please God.

that we have a strong desire to matter. We really, really, really want life to have purpose and meaning. This desire is so strong that even people who vehemently deny God's existence still live as if their lives matter.

Since I'm borrowing this idea from a writer named C.S. Lewis, I'll let him finish the thought:

> *Creatures are not born with desires unless satisfaction for these desires exists. A baby feels hunger; well, there is such a thing as food. A duckling wants to swim; well, there is such a thing as water. Men feel sexual desire; well, there is such a thing as sex. If I find in myself a desire which no experience in this world can satisfy, the most probable explanation is that I was made for another world.* [3]

Now it would be too big of a stretch to take that desire for purpose and conclude, "There is a God, and He wrote the Bible, and sent His Son Jesus." But it's a pointer. And it's a pointer we all seem to share.

Another pointer we all seem to share is that we all think bigger than dirt should.

I took my daughter Sierra to Italy after she graduated from high school. We saw a lot of wonderful things, but there were a few things we wanted to see and didn't. Like Michelangelo's *David* in Florence or his *Pieta* in Rome. Those didn't work out. The line to St. Peter's Basilica, where the *Pieta* resides, was so long we figured we could see dozens of things in the time we spent waiting to see it. And in Florence, we didn't check on the line because the price of admission to the museum was prohibitive for our budget (plus there's a replica on top of a hill in Florence and it's free).

A good question to ask here is why are people waiting for hours in line in the hot sun to see the *Pieta*, and paying beaucoup bucks to see statues? I mean, when it comes down to it aren't they just rocks with strategic portions cut away?

Well, no. It seems we humans have identified this thing we

---

[3] C.S. Lewis, *Mere Christianity*, Bk. III, chap. 10, "Hope"

9

call beauty, and while it makes no sense that clumps of dirt in transition would care about the rock left after one clump of dirt took a chisel to a bigger rock, or the way crystalized frozen water falls to the ground (and just lies there), or how light rays refract to create colorful illusions as the sun sets, we do. We care a lot. And while it's hard to explain if we're merely dirt in transition in a universe without God, it makes a lot of sense if we live in a universe created by a God who appreciates beauty and created humans with the capacity to do the same.

And finally,[4] there's the fact that we all wish we had the ability to zap.

Admit it. If you could have any ability that we frequently assign to deities, it's the zapping thing we really wish we could do. I mean, who wouldn't be zapping child molesters into piles of charcoal if we had the ability? When you see the news stories about people who abuse dozens of animals, keeping them in tiny cages, ignoring festering sores and constant whines, don't you wish the earth would just open up and swallow the abuser? On a petty level, we even secretly desire to administer at least a little jolt to the guy or gal who cuts in front of us in the line at the movie theater.

Here comes the big problem. Where do we get that universal belief that there are things that are wrong, and that violating those basic principles should result in punishment? Why do we clumps of dirt get upset when someone we know is guilty gets off scot-free, or when we learn an innocent person has been punished?

If we are mere dirt in transition, there really isn't a good explanation. But if we are something else, if the answer to the question, "What am I?" is somehow tied to a God who really exists and values justice, then it could make perfect sense that

---

[4] "Finally" for the sake of our discussion. There are lots more pointers we could look at, but the purpose of this section is to show there is a solid, rational foundation for faith, not to uncover every aspect of that foundation. If you want to learn more, check out the additional resources in the Appendix.

I lose my cool over child abusers or animal abusers or even bold-faced line busters.

Practicing Your Penmanship

In order for you to write your faith in your own handwriting, you can't just read what I write. You have to think it through, process it for yourself, and decide what you think about what you've read. At the end of some chapters, I'm including questions to help you think through what you've read and start to apply it to your own life. Also, if you're reading this book with a group, these questions can quick-start your discussion.

1. We looked at three primary concepts that point toward God, our own self-awareness, beauty, and our desire for justice? Do you find one more convincing than the others? Which one and why?

2. What other reasons can you think of that lead you to believe there must be more to life than just the accidental results of a physical universe?

3. How do you think you would (or should) behave differently if you truly believe you are more than dirt in transition?

2 THE PARADOX THAT EXPLAINS (ALMOST) EVERYTHING

I can hear the objections. Sure, I have a desire to zap child molesters, but how could a good God allow child molesters in the first place? If God really thinks His creation is good, how could He let us screw it up this badly, and mistreat His animals so viciously?

Honestly, I don't fully know. But the fact that I can't explain that piece doesn't help the person who wants to deny the existence of God. My, "I don't know why God allows everything He does" is still a better answer than "Clumps of self-aware dirt accidentally acquired the ability to care deeply about helpless animals and sex-trafficked Cambodian children."

See, I don't think Christianity explains everything perfectly. I just think its explanations make more sense than anything else. Or, as C.S. Lewis put it, "I believe in Christianity as I believe that the sun has risen: not only because I see it, but because by it I see everything else."[5] I think the world is clearer and makes more sense through the glasses of Christian faith than through any other set of lenses.

One big reason I believe this is because of two conflicting truths that do a better job of explaining humans than any other explanation I've seen. The first explains why we admire beauty and long for justice. The second explains why we destroy beauty and commit injustices.

---

[5] This quote was originally Lewis' final statement in the lecture "Is Theology Poetry?" presented on November 6, 1944, to the Oxford Socratic Club. It was published in the essay collection *They Asked for a Paper* (1962), among others.

We Are God's Image Bearers.

So God created human beings in his own image. In the image of God he created them; male and female he created them. Then God blessed them and said, "Be fruitful and multiply. Fill the earth and govern it. Reign over the fish in the sea, the birds in the sky, and all the animals that scurry along the ground." [6]

Christian faith teaches that the truest thing about humans is that they bear the amazing characteristic of somehow being the very image of God. This image makes us different from every other creature and explains so much about us.

First, we are self-aware. We contemplate our existence in ways dogs and cats and gorillas and dolphins just don't and can't.

Second, we need to be needed. We want to have a purpose, a meaning for our existence, again in a way animals do not. If you look closely at the section of Genesis I quoted above, you'll see that's why we get upset about mistreated animals. Part of our purpose and meaning for existence is to take care of the creation, including the animals. We get upset about mistreated animals because it strikes at the heart of who we were created to be.

Finally, and probably most importantly, the image of God in us means we were created for a relationship with God.

In our garage there is a large, plastic tote full of electronics, mainly chargers. We've kept every charger we've ever had. Why? Well, while almost every one of them is identical on one end (the prongs that plug into the wall), what comes out the other end is always different. There are large round plugs and small ones; USB plugs and mini-USB and micro-USB and squarish plugs and… well, a whole tote full of different plugs.

But why keep them all? Because each one only works with a certain type of jack. The USB jack on my laptop won't take

---

[6] Genesis 1:27-28 (NLT)

mini-USB, let alone some round or square plug. And because we are made in the image of God, we have the equivalent of a God jack. A part of us that has needs that can only be met by connecting with God, even though we try to satisfy it with everything but.

That God-likeness explains beauty and justice. It explains Mother Teresa and why we love sunsets. It explains why we desire so much more than dirt in transition ever rationally could, and why we long for things that this universe seems incapable of providing.

But what about serial killers and hate blogs and Adam Sandler movies? Where does that come from?

That's the second of the two conflicting truths.

We Are Fallen Creatures

The truest thing about us is that we are made in the image of God. The second truest thing is that we are rebellious, fallen creatures who reject God and His ways. The image of God is taught in Genesis chapters one and two, the first two chapters in the Bible. Our "fallenness" is taught in chapter three.

According to Genesis 3, humanity had a choice to live as God directed, or to rebel. We rebelled. And that rebellion has echoed throughout our history, affecting almost everything about us, blurring the image, and explaining the things about us that the image of God does not.

For instance, while we were created for a relationship with God, all of us find this challenging. The best of us struggles to maintain the connection and live God's principles. It seems fallenness is hereditary. We are inherently corrupt creatures. We are screwed up.

Now some people say humans are inherently good and are corrupted by adults and environment. These people apparently do not have children. I have three wonderful daughters. But as much as I love them, the fact is I didn't have to teach them to do wrong. They figured out how to lie and throw tantrums and steal their sisters' cookies with no assistance from their mother or me. Our struggle—as is every parent's—was the opposite. The challenge was teaching them to do good and resist the bad.

This fallenness impacts everything about us. It interferes with our relationships with other people. It leads to shame, and even spreads out into all of creation, as we find ourselves destroying the thing we were created to sustain.[7]

But here's the thing. It doesn't negate the image of God in us. It merely blurs it. So we strive to be noble creatures while self-sabotaging. We fight to make the world a better place, but often find selfish desires providing just as much motivation as the noble ones. We do good—and hope someone was watching and will reward us for it.

Which leaves us with a big problem. How do we reconcile those two parts of ourselves, and possibly even more importantly, how do we move into a relationship with God while still carrying around this fallen nature?

Well, Christianity proposes a unique solution to that one, too.

---

[7] We'll dig into this more deeply in the third section of the book.

3 THE CHRISTIAN SOLUTION

The conflicting concepts of our being fallen image-bearers provides the best path to understanding ourselves. Similarly, the solution to our biggest problem comes from following that same seemingly-contradictory path.

The fallen part means we are incapable of getting to God on our own. We can turn over a garden's worth of new leaves, but we're still the same. Screwed up. And the sense of justice within us only compounds the problem. We do things that we know are wrong, and we know wrongs should be punished.

Punished how? We may not be sure, but the punishment we observe and live out every day is separation from God. The Bible talks about how that separation will play out after death, but our own experience tells us we're living that separation right now. Each of us is drawn toward God (or "the Divine" or something greater than ourselves). And none of us are able to honestly believe that we've fully reached Him on our own no matter how hard we try. Religion turns to empty ritual. Doing good makes us feel good about ourselves, for a while, but the feelings fade and we still aren't any closer to God.

Bottom line: We cannot get to God.

So, because He created us for a relationship with Him, He came to us.

From the beginning, Christians have believed that Jesus was God in human form.[8] "In the beginning was the Word,

---

[8] There are some who deny it, but the evidence is extremely strong that the earliest church believed Jesus was God.

and the Word was made flesh and dwelt among us."[9] He then lived a non-screwed-up life, not sinning in any way.

We experience separation from God because of our sins. If God doesn't step in, we will also experience death and eternal separation from Him as the ultimate payment for our sin.

But Jesus didn't sin, so He was never separated from God and didn't have to pay the debt of death for His own sin. That means if He died, it would not be for His own sins, but for someone else's.

Now, if Jesus had been merely human, He could have then died as a substitute for one person. But being God, He was able to carry the debt of all humanity with Him to the cross. So He took all our sin debt on Himself and died on a cross, paying our penalty, then rose from the dead (which is a really big deal), to prove He has the power to deal with all our sin and to connect us with God.

If you were paying close attention, you may have noticed that we are merely passive spectators in that whole section. God in Jesus did it all. Our job is not to work our way to God (which we've learned we can't do), but to accept what Jesus has done and move into the relationship that God created us for in the first place.

Of course, there is the elephant in the room. I snuck it in without even giving it its own full sentence: "then rose from the dead (which is a really big deal)...." Choosing to follow Jesus includes one minor challenge. Believing the impossible.

See, I've encountered plenty of dead people. None of them got over it. But the Bible says that if Jesus didn't really, literally rise from the dead, Christianity is a joke and we're all wasting our time.[10] But how in the world can anyone be expected to believe the impossible?

Well, we'll start with an assumption (one that makes a lot of sense): God can do anything He wants. It's part of the

---

[9] John 1:1, 14
[10] 1 Corinthians 15:14

whole "being God" thing. With that in mind, the question becomes, "Is there enough evidence to believe that God overcame the laws of His own physical universe to raise Jesus from the dead?"

Obviously, I believe the answer is yes. While entire books have been written to justify that belief, there is one primary reason I accept it: the way the disciples acted afterward.

On the day Jesus was crucified, the disciples were scared and scattered. They feared for their own lives and denied they even knew who Jesus was.[11] After the crucifixion, things didn't immediately get any better. They were discouraged and looking for ways to get back to their previous lives.[12]

But then something happened. A few days later they were boldly proclaiming Jesus was alive again and asking others to join the cause. Thousands did.

Then the persecution came. The followers were threatened with death if they didn't recant what they were teaching, specifically that Jesus rose from the dead.

But instead of recanting this impossibility, they died. Stephen, an early follower, was stoned to death. Then James, one of Jesus' inner circle, was beheaded. Eventually every one of Jesus' closest followers, and many of his second-level followers, were given the choice of denial or death. None denied. Before the alleged resurrection, plenty of Jesus' followers walked away. None did after.

Matter of fact, the ones who actually witnessed the resurrection were so convincing in their lives and deaths that many of their followers were also willing to die for what they'd been taught—and because of their personal, spiritual encounters with the resurrected Jesus.

So many early Christians were willing to die for the resurrected Jesus that the meaning of a Greek word changed. Originally, it simply meant "to witness," as in to appear in court and testify something happened. But so many people

---

[11] Matthew 26:69-74

[12] Luke 24:13-21; John 21:3

who bore witness to the resurrected Jesus were killed that the meaning of that word changed, too. Now the word "martyr" is more about dying for what you believe than witnessing to it.

All because the people who claimed to have witnessed the resurrection held to their belief with so much passion they were willing to die for it.

Now, I know some people who will vehemently defend a lie. But I've never known anyone who would die for one. And I definitely don't know hundreds who would die for what they knew to be a lie. So, the earliest followers truly believed Jesus rose from the dead. And the best explanation for why that many people believed it so strongly is that Jesus really rose from the dead and appeared to them. No other explanation comes close to explaining it. Because of their passionate commitment, (along with some other evidences) I also believe that Jesus really rose from the dead.

If the resurrection actually happened, it also follows that the new life He offers to us is real and available. He gives us the opportunity for that connection with God we were created for.

And I believe that He offers it to everyone who simply believes and accepts it, just like His early followers said.[13]

Sounds simple, doesn't it?

Then why doesn't everybody accept it?

I think there are two obstacles. Ironically, neither is directly about Jesus.

The first obstacle is that deciding to be a Christian starts with admitting an uncomfortable truth: I'm screwed up. The theological phrase is, I'm a sinner. I do things that are wrong, I do them on purpose, and I'll probably do them again. That means I cannot get to God on my own.

It also means that to accept what God did for me in Jesus, I have to fully own up to who I am (which involves admitting my own guilt), quit trying to get to God on my own, and trust

---

[13] John 1:12

Him enough to change my life's direction and follow Him. That change of direction is called repentance, and it's hard to set aside our pride enough to make that difficult step. We're good at trusting ourselves. We're lousy at trusting anyone else—especially a God we can't see.

But that's the path God laid out, and that path of trusting Him instead of ourselves keeps some people from ever accepting God's love.

The second obstacle is even less about Jesus. It's about the Church. I've rarely met anyone who rejects Jesus. I've met tons who reject His followers and their wacky and/or offensive beliefs. Many people don't want to write the Christian faith in their own handwriting because of some of the things they believe they'll have to include in their document.

So, in the next section, we'll dig into the beliefs that are truly "required" to call yourself a Christian. You're probably going to be surprised. Whether you're checking out Christianity from a skeptical perspective or have been a Christian your whole life, you'll most likely learn a few things.

Hopefully, you'll see that being a Christian and writing the faith in your own handwriting isn't as whacky and offensive as some people make it appear.

Practicing Your Penmanship

1. What have you seen people who call themselves Christians do that make you not want to be categorized with them?

2. It's not hard to think of ways people show their fallenness. Are there areas of your own life where you are especially aware you are screwed up?

3. People don't always act like they are made in the image of God, but sometimes when they do, it's quite noticeable. Name a few times you've seen people act in ways that make it hard to consider them mere dirt in transition.

4. How hard is it for you to believe that Jesus really rose from the dead? If it's true, what difference do you think it should make in how you view the world? What difference should it make in how you live your life?

Part 2:
The Basics of Faith

4 SEEKING TRUTH

So, there was this fight on Facebook. It started as a discussion, but pretty soon tempers flared, words were being typed UPPERCASE (which is internet for yelling), and people were being unfriended left and right.

What happened?

Believe it or not, it really wasn't about the issue being debated. It was about the assumptions behind the positions the people held on the issue. Most of the time, our biggest disagreements are never voiced—or even acknowledged.

See, there are three levels of understanding.[14] The first level is how we answer the Big Questions: Is there a God? (Yes, no, don't know.) If yes, is there just one? Is Jesus His Son? Was Jesus just a great teacher, or did He die for our sins? The first section of the book was about these questions, because how you answer the big questions determines how you'll deal with the next two levels: knowledge and decisions.

The Knowledge Level is about how we process and rank the information. How much can we trust our senses? Do we let our emotions influence our judgements? Are the findings of science reliable, applicable, or even relevant? How much should we let the Bible (or some form of divine revelation) impact our actions? And, if there is a conflict within the information, what overrules what? Do emotions trump logic, or vice versa?

Unfortunately, few people are even aware of this level of knowledge. For most, these are assumptions they take for granted instead of concepts they have intentionally processed. So, when we get to the third level … fireworks!

---

[14] The philosophical term for what we're about to discuss is "epistemology."

See, at the Decision Level, we take the inputs we receive, rank them according to the assumptions we've made at the Knowledge Level, and come to conclusions we apply to life. Often passionately.

One person presents what they believe to be a highly logical argument (if they believe logic is a valid approach to knowledge). The second person responds with what makes perfect sense—to them.

The first person leans a little closer and repeats their argument. The second leans in and repeats theirs. The first then decides the second isn't really hearing them, so they increase their volume. The second responds in kind. Soon both sides are just yelling, and no one is making any progress toward agreement.

So, we end up with anti-vaccinators, people who don't trust the findings of the scientific establishment, screaming at scientifically-aware pro-vaccinators. The blood pressure of people who believe all humans are made in the image of God spikes, because people who don't even believe in God won't come around to their way of thinking. And religious fanatics, who think God has given them every jot and tittle of truth, wave placards of hate at everyone who disagrees with them.

This section of the book will be examining the second level of knowledge—how we acquire and rank the information we need to make decisions. Specifically, we'll be looking at how the God we discussed in the first section reveals truth to us, how we should value that revelation, and what it really means to us as we attempt to write our faith in our own handwriting.

Along the way, we'll uncover the core truths that are essential to Christianity. We'll also examine some other beliefs that might be as dependent on how we choose to process the available information as they are about what the Bible says.

The Need for Revelation

Of course, some might ask, why do we need the Bible? Between all the other sources of information, couldn't God get us all the data we need without going to the trouble of creating a book? Especially a book written by dozens of authors over the course of centuries?

Well, once again it goes back to those two conflicting truths—we are fallen and we are the image of God, with an emphasis this time on the fallen part.

For instance, our emotions are powerful—and incredibly flawed. Have you ever been really worked up about something only to find out it was a misunderstanding? Scientists really seek out truth. They also really have biases that can potentially impact their findings. And we have biases for or against scientists. Our senses don't even always get it right. Is the dress blue or gold,[15] does the bar really bend when it enters the water, and is that rainbow really there or just an illusion?

What we need is something that will reveal truths we couldn't get on our own, and provide a straight line to determine which inputs are accurate and which are skewed by our fallenness. And so we come to revelation.

---

[15] Remember the Internet sensation of the dress that some people saw as blue and black, while others saw as white and gold?
http://www.wired.com/2015/02/science-one-agrees-color-dress

5 REVEALED TRUTH

When it comes to faith, we live in a salad-bar culture. Just pick and choose whatever you want from whatever source you choose. Can't find anything you like? Just make something up.

Which would be perfectly fine, if there wasn't a God who speaks. But if there really is a God, and He really has communicated with us, then everything changes. Matter of fact, if God chose to be a malevolent dictator who wants to make our lives miserable, we'd really have little choice but to obey.

Thankfully, that doesn't seem to be the case. It seems that God has spoken through Jesus, and what He spoke doesn't seem mean at all. Matter of fact, one of my favorite Jesus sayings is, "My purpose is to give them a rich and satisfying life."[16] And the "them" He's talking about is us.

So, how do we know what He says? It's not as complicated as it sounds. It seems He's spoken through three primary sources.

The first, obviously, is Jesus. If He really rose from the dead (see last section for that), that resurrection validates everything about Him. (I can't imagine God letting a charlatan rise from the dead.)

When the Bible's Book of Hebrews talks about Jesus, it says this: "In the past God spoke to our ancestors through the prophets at many times and in various ways, but in these last days he has spoken to us by his Son, whom he appointed heir of all things, and through whom also he made the universe. The Son is the radiance of God's glory and the

---

[16] John 10:10 (NIV)

exact representation of his being, sustaining all things by his powerful word."[17] Which is pretty heady stuff.

That verse points us to the second way we can learn about God, His creation. In a very real sense, the universe is God's work of art, and art always reflects, in some way, the nature of its creator. Or Creator. Dating back to well before Jesus, people of faith have believed that we can learn about God from what we see in nature. "The heavens proclaim the glory of God. The skies display his craftsmanship. Day after day they continue to speak; night after night they make him known."[18]

And of course, the third way Christians have always believed that God communicates is through the Bible. Now, we're not just taking this as some illogical leap of faith. We have very good reasons for believing that the Bible is speaking the truth about itself when it says that it was in some metaphysical way actually breathed by God.[19]

For one thing, while people have attacked it pretty much since it was written, it has stood the test of time. When it speaks, it seems to speak accurately. When it speaks of history, it gets it right. For many years, people discredited the Bible because it spoke of a city called Nineveh, which no one could find. Until archaeologists finally found it, and it matched what was written about it in amazing detail. Matter of fact, the Bible has been shown to be so accurate when it comes to geography and archaeology that it's basically the starting point to finding ancient sites throughout the Near East.

But probably more importantly, it's accurate when it talks about us. No book describes the human condition more honestly and accurately than the Bible. The Book of James refers to it as a mirror, and as someone who's spent decades reading it, I can say I see myself in it much more frequently

---

[17] Hebrews 1:1-3 (NIV)

[18] Psalm 19:1-2 (NLT)

[19] 2 Timothy 3:16

than I'd like.

To push it a step further, for most people who've spent their lives experiencing the Bible, its accuracy is beyond anything a human could accomplish. It certainly seems that the books that make up the Bible are in fact inspired. "Prophets, though human, spoke from God as they were carried along by the Holy Spirit,"[20] is how the Bible itself refers to it.

Of course, some people could accurately accuse me of circular reasoning. Using the Bible to say the Bible is accurate and inspired is logically weak. Saying it's inspired because I feel it to be so doesn't separate it from dozens of other books that help people feel more spiritual.

It would help to have a witness that had a little more authority than someone who makes his living saying the book he teaches is authoritative.

So let's go back to the Resurrection. See, it's not just that I say the Bible is the word of God, Jesus said it, too. Time after time He prefaced an argument by saying "It is written." In other words, He believed the Bible spoke with the authority of God. Jesus even said, "For truly I tell you, until heaven and earth disappear, not the smallest letter, not the least stroke of a pen, will by any means disappear from the Law until everything is accomplished."[21]

And He's the one who rose from the dead. So when the guy who rose from the dead says the Bible is the result of God speaking, I'm on solid ground to take His word for it.

But Which Books?

Before we go any further, we probably should spend a little bit of time on an objection people love to make. What about the books the church left out of the Bible? It seems every few months some publication is trumpeting a book that was too controversial to be included in the Bible. After all,

---

[20] 2 Peter 1:21 (NIV)
[21] Matthew 5:18 (NIV)

didn't they just pick the books they liked?

Well, in a word, no.

We can start with the Old Testament, the books of the Bible that predate Jesus. The technical word for the list of accepted books is "canon," and the Jewish canon was firmly established well before Jesus came on the scene.

As for the New Testament, it was primarily about connection and voice.

First, how did the book connect back to Jesus? If one of the original disciples wrote it, that was definitely a plus. Most of these "lost books" that are promoted now were written hundreds of years after Jesus, and had at best tenuous connections with the earliest followers. Every book that is in the New Testament can be dated to within one hundred years of Jesus, most much closer than that. Those books that keep getting mentioned as having been left out of the Bible? Almost all were written more than a hundred years after the youngest book in the Bible. Some are over 500 years younger.

If you dig into it, you'll find that the books that have the best claims to having been "left out" don't contain any wild teachings. They're right in line with what the included books say. Matter of fact, some even reinforce traditional church teachings that aren't stated as explicitly in the New Testament.[22] These books weren't passed over as much because of teaching or connection as because they failed the second test, the voice test.

To understand the voice test, imagine you have travelled to Ghana to adopt a child. You visit an orphanage and are taken to a large room where all the children are playing. What are you looking for as you tackle the challenge of choosing which child to take home? Bright eyes? High energy? Not-so-high energy?

Okay, let's change the scenario. Let's say you didn't just choose Ghana as the best of many options. Let's say you had

---

[22] For instance, *Didache* and *The Epistle of Barnabas* both teach specifically against performing abortions.

a sister, whom you had lost touch with a few years ago. Recently, you discovered that your sister moved to Ghana, married a man, and had two children. Unfortunately, both she and her husband were killed in a car crash. Their two daughters have been placed in an orphanage and you have travelled to Ghana to find them, bring them home, and raise them.

Now what are you looking for? "That one has my sister's eyes." "Doesn't that sound like her laugh?" "She runs just like my sister!"

That's what the early church was looking for when it came to the canon of the New Testament. They had listened to authentic teachers, read books they had no doubt been inspired by God, and heard God's voice speak into their lives. They were listening for that same voice in the books they considered including in the New Testament.

I started reading the Bible regularly when I was in fifth grade. I read at least a chapter a day from fifth grade through twelfth. Along the way I heard about these "lost books." When I went to college, I decided to find some of them and read them. So, I went to the library, checked out some of these books, and started reading a chapter a day, just like I'd done for years.

I kept it up for about a week. It just didn't work. I wasn't offended by them. (The regular Bible has plenty to offend me.) There was something missing. Unknowingly, I'd done exactly what the early church had done. I recognized certain books didn't belong in the Bible, not because there was something wrong, but because there was something missing—the voice of God.

For the early church, books that had that strong connection with Jesus and spoke with the voice of God were included in the Bible. Those that didn't, weren't. No conspiracy, just striving for consistency.

Practicing Your Penmanship

1. Do you ever feel closer to God in nature than in other settings? Name something you have learned about God by observing nature.

2. Is there anything you observe in nature that could lead you to thinking something inaccurate about God? (Example: The way animals eat other animals could lead someone to believe God is uncaring.)

3. Does it make sense to you that we need specific revelation like the Bible? What is your biggest obstacle to believing the Bible is what it claims to be?

4. Have you ever believed God was speaking to you through the Bible, or have you ever felt moved by what you read in the Bible?

6 THE DEFINING PAIR

So far, we've established two crucial teachings in Christianity. First, Jesus really rose from the dead. Second, the Bible is the accurate, authoritative, inspired[23] word of God.[24]

As I was preparing for this book, I noticed something. These two major points provide a great test for what teachings are crucial to Christianity and which are at some level secondary.

What I saw was this: There are certain teachings that pretty much 100% of people who believe these two things agree on. But if you add even the slightest detail to these teachings, the percentages drop drastically.

For instance, obviously 100% of these people believe that the Bible is the word of God. But if you add in any questions about which translation, or what translation philosophy should be prioritized, or even which Greek texts should be used to translate the New Testament, not a single view is claimed by a majority of the Church.

As we mentioned in the first major section, we believe that Jesus died for our sins. 100% of the people who believe Jesus rose from the dead, and that the Bible is the accurate, authoritative, inspired word of God believe this. But did He die for all humanity, or just those who believe? Can anyone

---

[23] Many people try to find a single word to encompass these three words. Some of these single words don't quite hit the mark specifically enough, while others have become politically loaded in one denomination or another. I just try to skip the controversy and use three words instead of one to define the concept.

[24] Also, some denominations (including Catholicism) apply these concepts with an additional factor: as interpreted by the Church. If it helps you to add that proviso, I'm fine with it but don't want to spend more than a footnote discussing it.

choose to believe, or are all believers chosen by God ahead of time? Once a person follows Jesus, can they walk away and lose their relationship with God? The percentages nose dive when we get to each of those questions.

This makes it very easy to identify the truly crucial, core teachings about Christianity. Does everyone who believes that Jesus rose from the dead and that the Bible is the accurate, authoritative, inspired word of God believe it? If yes, then it's a core teaching of Christianity. If not, each of us may consider it important, and it might be a very important question (many of them are), but it's not central to Christianity.

Obviously, if we're going to write the Christian faith in our own handwriting, it's vitally important that we distinguish between the universal core truths (like Jesus died for our sins) from the secondary truths (like how much influence we have in choosing to follow).

So we'll proceed with the belief that a core truth is anything believed by basically 100% of the people who believe in Resurrection and Revelation (which I'm going to start typing instead of inspired, accurate, and authoritative). Everything else, no matter how crucial the question, is secondary at best.

An especially interesting case to understand this principle is the first one we'll look at here.

7 GOD AND TRINITY

Trinity means that God is somehow three and one at the same time. There is only one God, and He exists somehow as three distinct persons—that are still one. Confusing, huh?

Here's the thing. That God exists in Trinity is universally agreed upon. When doing the "who believes it" survey, basically 100% of the people who agree on Revelation and Resurrection believe in the Trinity. This is surprising for two reasons. First, it is the least explicitly taught of all the core truths. The Bible specifically says that Jesus died for our sins at least six times.[25] There is not a single passage that explicitly teaches the Trinity.[26]

The second reason the Trinity is a surprising core teaching is that no one understands it. I mean, no one.

The Trinity is easily the most confusing Bible teaching. We believe that there is one God, but that one God exists in three distinct persons, Father, Son (Jesus), and Holy Spirit. God the Father is God. Jesus is God. The Holy Spirit is God. But Jesus is not the Holy Spirit, nor God the Father. God the Father is not the Holy Spirit. (Mathematically speaking, the transitive property does not apply to the Godhead.)

Or to put it another way (that is still confusing), God the Father, Jesus, and the Holy Spirit are three distinct persons who share one identical essence or nature. Not similar essences or natures, like say identical twins might, but one identical essence. They are one and cannot be divided.

And it is beyond our human brains to understand it. Not

---

[25] Romans 4:25; 1 Corinthians 15:3; Galatians 1:4; Titus 2:14; Hebrews 9:28; 1 Peter 2:24

[26] In some translations, 1 John 5:7-8 seems to imply it, but even that isn't explicit.

to say we haven't tried. For two thousand years we've been trying, coming up with analogy after analogy. The Trinity is like an egg (yolk, white, shell), water (water, ice, steam), a woman (mother, daughter, granddaughter). But each falls apart on closer inspection.

We accept the Trinitarian nature of God because the Bible teaches it. Even if there isn't a verse that proclaims Trinity, or even a verse that uses the word, the teaching is clear. There are numerous times where two or even all three are acting simultaneously or mentioned together as individuals,[27] and also numerous times they are each declared to be God.[28] even as the Bible declares definitively that God is One.[29]

Nevertheless, the teaching on the Trinity has been universally declared from the earliest days of the church, with the only debate being about proper definition and defense, not whether or not it was true.

The question you might be asking is, if it's so confusing, why is it considered so crucial? I think there are two primary reasons. One, to understand Jesus, we have to understand Him as Divine, as God. The Trinity is the path to helping us make sense (even if confusing sense) of Jesus as truly the Son of God.

Secondly, and more practically, it explains something about the universe that other faiths (and non-faiths) have trouble with: relationships. How does a non-related God produce creatures that thrive on relationships? Do we have a quality God lacks, and how could God give us something He doesn't possess? If there is no God, how do clumps of dirt form relationships, and why does dirt in transition hurt so much when relationships are broken?

But God as Trinity is a God of relationships. He is related within Himself, and as His image bearers, we are created for relationships. The Trinity may be a confusing idea, but it

---

[27] John 14:6; Matthew 3:16-17; Matthew 28:19; 2 Corinthians 13:14, for instance.

[28] A couple of examples: John 1:1, 14; Acts 5:3-4.

[29] Deuteronomy 6:4; Jeremiah 10:6

makes it easier to understand why relationships are so crucial to our existence.

God

Now that you're fully confused about God, let's take things back a notch to things that are still pretty much universally accepted, but will make our heads hurt a little bit less. To do this, we'll want to talk about God's perfections. This brings up to two immediate questions. What is a "perfection," and why should thinking about God's nature make our heads hurt at all?

First, about perfections. Some people call them qualities or attributes, but I prefer the word perfections. An illustration should help. God is love. You could call it one of God's qualities, but you could also say that some humans have that same quality. God doesn't just possess the quality of love or the ability to love. God personifies love. He is the ultimate example of love. It is an intrinsic part of who He is, and He is the perfect embodiment of love. Though we cannot always understand it, God's every action is loving, because love is ultimately a reflection of who He truly is. In other words, it is one of His perfections.

But why should thinking deeply about God's perfections make my head hurt? Well, that's because one of His perfections is that He is ineffable, a word you've probably never heard and don't understand. That's okay, because that means you've almost got it. Ineffable means incapable of being expressed or described in words. God is so big, so amazing, so, well, just SO, that human words can't get close to capturing His essence.

When God appeared to Moses at the burning bush, Moses asked Him for His name. God replied, *"I AM WHO I AM. This is what you are to say to the Israelites: 'I AM has sent me to you.'"*[30] In other words, Don't even try to pin me down with a

---

[30] Exodus 3:14 (NIV)

35

name. I am beyond all your words. (By the way, that "I am who I am" is where we get the word Jehovah or Yahweh.)

Thankfully, God has some perfections that are easier to express in words, even if His totality is beyond words. For instance, God is self-existent, self-sufficient and self-sustaining. That means He doesn't need us, He's never needed anyone, and He never will.[31] As Aristotle figured out without even seeing the Bible, God is the Unmoved Mover who causes all things without being caused by anything.[32]

God is also holy, loving, and morally perfect. On the surface, that one sounds almost like a cheat. If God is the definition of love, and morals are defined by His nature, then of course He's loving and moral. And if holiness is being separated from things that are opposed to God, well, again pretty obvious. But there is an underlying perfection that makes this less of a truism. See, God is good. Not good because He defines good, but good because He is greater than anything we could imagine. And if God's love wasn't pure and his morality wasn't the best possible morality, I could imagine a greater good than God.

We won't try to dig into all of God's perfections. People have written entire books on that subject, but we'll finish up this section with another head scratcher that should also make you very happy. Along the way, this could help you understand one reason churches can be so different. God is both *transcendent over*, and *immanent in*, His world. Transcendent means God is "totally other." We've already said He is ineffable, but He is also untouchable. We can't change Him, understand Him, or do much more than stand in awe of Him.

But He is also immanent. You may have noticed that immanent sounds a lot like Immanuel from the Christmas songs (and Isaiah 7:14). That's not a coincidence. "El" on the end of an Old Testament word frequently means "God", so

---

[31] Acts 17:24-25
[32] https://en.wikipedia.org/wiki/Unmoved_mover

Immanuel means God (El) is with us (immanent). God has chosen to dwell with us, to be among us, to speak with us, to act in our world. He is here.

And that explains why there are two primary types of churches. Some people worship God best by contemplating His transcendence, His awesome otherness. Incense and stained glass and robes and liturgies remind them that God is beyond their comprehension and worthy of worship.

Others worship best by focusing on the nearness of God. He is here; He is my friend; He walks with me, and He talks with me. He is a comforting presence more than a thundering voice.

Which is the proper way to worship? Well, I personally believe that we need both. The God who is greater than I can imagine chooses to dwell with (and in[33]) me. But this is a classic example of writing your faith in your own handwriting. You can worship God in a cathedral with Gregorian chants, and you can worship God by a campfire with a strumming guitar. The real question is how do you worship God best? What excites you, moves you, and makes your worship most authentic? What best reinvigorates you so you can live out your faith after you leave the church service? Jesus said to worship God in Spirit and in truth.[34] I don't think it's stretching that saying too far to say it should include remaining true to the person God created you to be.

Practicing Your Penmanship

1. Why do you think the Trinity is such an important teaching? Can you think of anything that would change about Christianity if we did not believe in the Trinity?

2. Does it make you feel better or worse that God is ineffable?[35] Or does it impact you at all? Contrast that belief with the idea that

---

[33] The Bible also teaches that when we decide to follow Jesus, God's Spirit actually comes into us. John 14:17; Acts 2:4; Romans 8:9.

[34] John 4:23-24

[35] incapable of being expressed or described in words

God is the ultimate perfection of love.

3. Between immanence (God is near) and transcendence (God is other), which comforts you most? Which do you think will better lead you to worship?

8 CREATION

How about we move on to something less likely to make our heads hurt, but more likely to lead to an argument? Creation.

"In the beginning, God created."[36]

The fun thing about this one is that it's a perfect example of our core-teachings idea. The basics about creation fit easily into the 100% category. The first things we'll talk about with creation are as universally accepted as any Bible teaching. As soon as we move slightly away from the core concepts we get to ideas that are incredibly controversial. But in this case, instead of just talking about what's 100% accepted, we'll look at some of the variation. Because (to mix metaphors), if you're going to write your faith in your own handwriting, it's good to know how broad the tent of Christianity actually is, especially in the contentious areas.

Let's start with the stuff we all agree on and a cool Latin phrase.

Ex Nihilo. That's Latin for "from nothing." It's actually a foundational belief in Christianity. There is a popular story about an atheist who issued a challenge to God. He claimed he could create life in a lab, making God unnecessary. He wanted God to come to his lab for a life-creation duel. God accepted, won the coin toss, and went first. He formed dirt into a pile, did some God stuff, and life sprouted from the dirt.

The atheist went next. He got his pile of dirt ready, but God interrupted. "Hey! Make your own dirt!"

That's the point of Creation *Ex Nihilo*. God didn't build

---

[36] Genesis 1:1

the universe from existing materials. We could say God created the materials out of thin air, but when He started there wasn't even thin air. Or even space for the thin air to occupy. Or time in which to do the construction. God created a space-time-stuff universe out of nothing. (I started to write, "where there was nothing," but again, there was no "where" for Him to do it. There was nothing in the purest sense of the word.)

Creation was also by His direction and for His purposes. Whatever method you believe God used to create, creation wasn't accidental. God did it on purpose and for His purposes. One of those purposes was to produce worshippers and other beings to be with Him, but also and ultimately to bring glory to Himself. I know that sounds narcissistic, but if you're the ultimate of perfection, pointing people to yourself isn't narcissistic. It's the best possible thing for them. (You may want to take a second to mull on that one before moving on.)

Finally, and crucially, creation is distinct from God. God is present everywhere, but He isn't everything. Trees, rocks, animals, and people aren't parts of God; we're separate creations of His. He caused and maintains our existence,[37] but we exist apart from Him.

If you want to draw the lines as to why all these are crucial, creation *ex nihilo* points to God's omnipotence (He's all-powerful), and all-sufficient. It also speaks against any theory that places the universe as existing independent of God or existing eternally prior to God's action. That the universe was created at His direction and for His purposes is in opposition to any theory that the universe was purely accidental, random, or meaningless.

Oh, one more thing before we get to the controversial stuff. The creation is good.

This is important because throughout Church history there has been a school of thought that teaches that matter is

---

[37] Colossians 1:16-17; Acts 17:28; John 1:3

imperfect or even evil, and that our souls are somehow trapped in matter. According to this view, one of our ultimate goals is to be free of this imperfect material world and be purely spiritual beings. In the early days of the Church, this was known as Gnosticism, but it still exists today under many names (and frequently under no name at all, just an assumption that even sneaks into the Church).

But when God finished creating the physical universe, He said what He made was "very good."[38] And when He restores His creation, the result is still a physical universe with rivers, trees, and even cities.[39] We are not spiritual beings having a physical experience, contrary to what de Chardin said[40]. We are physical-spiritual beings, finding our fulfillment only as we fully experience both. Our purpose as humans includes both connecting with God and caring for God's creation.[41]

That gets us close to an area where not everyone is 100% on board, but it is not the best example of how Christians can agree on the core truths, but disagree on the specifics of that truth. To get into the real juicy disagreements, we'll need to look briefly at God's mechanism of creation.

See, while everyone who holds to the two key truths about the Bible and resurrection believe God created the universe out of nothing, you can get some real fireworks started by discussing how God did the creating.

Some people believe God created the universe in six 24-hour days roughly six to ten thousand years ago. This view is called Young-Earth Creationism. Some believe that God created the universe a long time ago, possibly in stages, but each species was created individually. This is Old-Earth Creationism, which usually allows for microevolution,

---

[38] Genesis 1:31

[39] Revelation 22:1-2; Revelation 21:2

[40] Pierre Teilhard de Chardin, the French philosopher, priest, and paleontologist, said, "We are not human beings having a spiritual experience. We are spiritual beings having a human experience," which is often misquoted by replacing the word "human" with "physical."

[41] Genesis 1:28

transition within species, but not macroevolution, transition from one species into another. The third primary view is Evolutionary Creationism, the belief that the universe is extremely old and that God utilized the mechanism of evolution to bring about life as we know it.

I'm not going to push for any of these views here,[42] but I do want to point out that there are many authentic Christians who believe each,[43] and many highly intelligent, committed Christians who admit to being unsure.[44] This diversity of opinion is basically as old as the church. You are allowed to do your own research, form your own conclusions, and still be well within the tent of the Christian faith.

But how can Christians arrive at such diverse opinions when they start with the same Bible? Glad you asked. It's a very important question.

And we'll deal with it in detail in Part 3, Your Faith.

Practicing Your Penmanship

1. Why do you think it matters whether God created the universe from nothing or it has always existed?
2. Do you have trouble with the idea that God created everything for His own glory? Can you see why it's different for us to try to call attention to ourselves than it is for God to call attention to Himself?
3. When have you heard someone say something like we are souls trapped in physical bodies? What would change about how you view life if you acknowledge that your physical presence is just as much "you" as your soul?
4. Does it bother you that Christians have such diverse views on such a foundational belief as Creation?

---

[42] I already wrote an entire book on the subject, so my view is readily available. *Evolving: My Journey to Reconcile Science and Faith.*

[43] I'd offer a list of names for each, but for many readers the names would mean nothing. It's not hard to do an internet search on the three approaches to get a lengthy list of names that you might recognize.

[44] The book *A Reformed Approach to Science and Scripture* was written to explain why uncertainty is a valid response. It's an excellent book even if you're not Reformed. And it's free. (Mine is $2.99.)

9 INVASION

The Bible is full of great stories. Adam and Eve. Noah and the Flood. Moses parting the Red Sea. The Battle of Jericho. David and Goliath. Jesus turning water into wine, and feeding thousands. Dozens of fascinating stories.

But amidst all those stories, people often miss a crucial idea. The Bible is using all those famous stories to tell one big story. The story of a God who created people in His own image, watched them rebel against Him, then set about doing whatever it took to restore both the people and His creation.

Adam and Eve begin the rebellion. Humanity gets a second chance with Noah. (We fail again. Quickly.) The Red Sea parts, and Jericho falls as God establishes a nation that He can use to begin His restoration project. David defeats Goliath, and puts himself in position to lead that nation, and also becomes the direct ancestor of the Rescuer humanity needs.

Jesus? Well, let's just say His primary purpose wasn't about either water or wine.

And it was all part of the plan.

The plan can even be seen in the curse that resulted from Adam and Eve's rebellion. Following their mutiny, the planet was cursed, men and women were cursed. Even the tempter was cursed.

But when God cursed the tempter, the curse contained a promise that kicked His plan into motion.

"I will cause hostility between you (the tempter) and the woman, and between your offspring and her offspring. He will

strike your head, and you will strike his heel."[45]

In case you didn't know, the He in question is Jesus, the One who crushed the power of death on the Cross.

It was all planned.

But when the fullness of time had come, God sent forth his Son.[46]

When God had everything laid out, He sent Jesus. The Romans built a basically safe road system heading west, the Persians constructed one heading east, and travel into Africa was just as secure. Knowing one or two key languages meant a person could communicate in much of the known world. Then when history was ready, God invaded.

Our picture is of a peaceful, silent night. It wasn't. It was war.

As we saw earlier, Jesus wasn't just a baby. He is part of the Trinity. Almighty God. Evil's only option was to kill Him. Which didn't really work out well for evil. It turned the Son of God loose on death.

Death lost.

And God's invasion is the most important piece of history.

Just like the other topics we've discussed, there are a few areas of disagreement when it comes to the invasion, but there are quite a few things that everyone who accepts Revelation and Resurrection agrees on. And like the Trinity, the most important thing is a concept that challenges our logic, but makes sense in its own way.

Incarnation

Basic logic says you can't be two things. My pet, Winter, isn't a dog **and** a hamster. He's a dog. Something can't be both a tree and an old man (even if Peter Jackson could create a convincing CGI version of the impossible in *The Lord of the Rings*).

---

[45] Genesis 3:15 (NLT)
[46] Galatians 4:4a (ESV)

Yet Jesus is both human and God.

Completely both.

We believe that Jesus was and is fully human.[47] He cooked and ate,[48] He got tired and slept.[49] He was even tempted.[50]

He also was and is fully God. This part troubles some people. People who deny Revelation and Resurrection frequently assert that Jesus being God was an idea that was hatched many years after Jesus' death, and that Jesus didn't believe it about Himself. Those ideas are hard to square with what we see in the Bible and Church history, though.

As for what the earliest Christians believed, there are numerous passages that proclaim the belief that Jesus is Divine.

The Son is the radiance of God's glory and the exact representation of his being, sustaining all things by his powerful word.[51]

So this biblical author believed Jesus was God, even ascribing to Him the job of holding the universe together. The same verse goes on to say,

After he had provided purification for sins, he sat down at the right hand of the Majesty in heaven.[52]

Sure sounds divine to me.

The Book of Colossians also has a fascinating take on Jesus.

For by him all things were created, in heaven and on earth, visible and invisible, whether thrones or dominions or rulers or authorities—all things were created through him and for him. And he is before all things, and in him all things hold

---

[47] Luke 24:39

[48] John 21:12-13

[49] Matthew 8:24-25

[50] Hebrews 4:15

[51] Hebrews 1:3 (NIV)

[52] *Ibid.*

together.[53]

Again we see the belief that Jesus holds the universe together (and probably spoke it into being). But what is most interesting about this passage is that most scholars don't think Paul, who wrote Colossians, wrote this. The consensus is that this is actually a hymn that Paul is quoting. In other words, it's older than the book of Colossians, meaning it was written before A.D. 62 or so. If you're doing the math, that means the song was written—and the ideas it proclaims accepted—less than 30 years after Jesus' death and resurrection. That's a very short time for an idea to crop up that is completely at odds with what the original followers believed. Especially since many of them were still alive.

And when you look at church history, you'll see that the early church had a lot more trouble understanding Jesus' humanity than His divinity. The three major groups that made up Christianity in the first thousand years after Christ had no trouble agreeing that Jesus was God, but they couldn't get together on how to make sense of His humanity.[54]

What about Jesus? Did He believe He was Divine?

One day Jesus was having (another) fight with the religious establishment. He finally got tired of the argument and said, "Truly, truly, I say to you, before Abraham was, I am."[55]

The first thing you might notice about that statement, is the tenses are weird. Before Abraham was (past tense), I am (present). It seems He's not just proclaiming that He was alive when Abraham was (which would make him about two thousand years old), but that He was pre-existent. That He had always existed.

But that's not the coolest part. Remember when we talked about God's perfections and brought up the idea that God is

---

[53] Colossians 1:16-17 (ESV)

[54] See the introductory materials to the book The Lost History of Christianity, section "A Note on Names and –isms". Kindle location 63. The three groups can be referred to as Orthodox or Catholic, Nestorians, and Jacobites.

[55] John 8:58 (ESV)

ineffable? The passage we quoted was when God appeared to Moses in a burning bush, and Moses asked God's name. Remember how God replied to that request?

"I AM WHO I AM. This is what you are to say to the Israelites: 'I AM has sent me to you.'"[56]

When Jesus said, "Before Abraham was, I AM," was Jesus claiming to be the voice that spoke from the bush? Well, we know how the religious people heard it. They believed Jesus was claiming to be God. We know this because of their response. They picked up rocks to stone Jesus to death for blasphemy.[57]

So, the early Church believed Jesus was fully God, Jesus believed it about Himself, and Christians ever since have bought into it.

In the beginning was the Word, and the Word was with God, and the Word was God. ... The Word became flesh and made his dwelling among us. We have seen his glory, the glory of the one and only Son, who came from the Father, full of grace and truth.[58]

Crucifixion and Resurrection

We've already discussed that idea that Jesus was both crucified and rose from the dead, but we probably should nail down a few ideas that accompany those events.

For instance, the Crucifixion and Resurrection were both real, physical events. Jesus didn't just pass out on the Cross, and then wake up in the tomb three days later. He died.

But when they came to Jesus, they saw that he was already dead, so they didn't break his legs. One of the soldiers, however, pierced his side with a spear, and immediately blood and water

---

[56] Exodus 3:14 (NIV)

[57] Jesus mysteriously slipped away to prevent a premature execution. John 8:59.

[58] John 1:1, 14 (NIV)

flowed out.[59]

One way we know He was really dead was the way His followers responded when He appeared to them. Pretend for a second that He'd merely passed out from the overwhelming abuse of the crucifixion. He then spent three days without food or water in a cave, bleeding, scabbing over, and getting weaker by the hour. Somehow He managed to roll the stone away from the tomb and stumble to the upstairs room where the disciples were meeting.

When this weakened, bloodied, limping man opened the door and stepped in, would His followers have called Him risen, or called for a doctor?[60]

We also believe that He was physically resurrected. That means it wasn't just a ghostly, spiritual presence the disciples saw. Matter of fact, when I was listing things Jesus did that showed Him to be human, many of the verses I used were from after the resurrection. And when Thomas missed the first appearance, Jesus offered Thomas the opportunity to touch his wounds as proof He was risen, just as He'd done for the ones who were there for that first appearance.

"Look at my hands and my feet. It is I myself! Touch me and see; a ghost does not have flesh and bones, as you see I have."[61]

Two more quick things about the Crucifixion and Resurrection. While they were physical actions, they had meaning well beyond the physical. He died as a substitute for us.

For Christ also suffered once for sins, the righteous for the unrighteous, that he might bring us to God, being put to death

---

[59] John 19:33-34 (NLT)

[60] Ironically, this refutation of the swoon theory was first proposed by a skeptic who didn't believe in the Resurrection, but recognized that this explanation was nonsense.

[61] Luke 24:39 (NIV)

in the flesh but made alive in the spirit.[62]

And that substitution was sufficient to re-connect us to God and bring us a new life now and forever.

For God so loved the world that he gave his one and only Son, that whoever believes in him shall not perish but have eternal life.[63]

I'll close this section with my favorite description of what Jesus' Crucifixion and Resurrection accomplished for us, from Paul's letter to Titus:

At one time we too were foolish, disobedient, deceived and enslaved by all kinds of passions and pleasures. We lived in malice and envy, being hated and hating one another. But when the kindness and love of God our Savior appeared, he saved us, not because of righteous things we had done, but because of his mercy. He saved us through the washing of rebirth and renewal by the Holy Spirit, whom he poured out on us generously through Jesus Christ our Savior, so that, having been justified by his grace, we might become heirs having the hope of eternal life.[64]

Practicing Your Penmanship

1. Which do you have the most trouble accepting, that Jesus was fully God, fully man, or that He existed at all? What evidence for each do you find most helpful?

2. Why do you think it is such a big deal that Jesus physically rose from the dead? What would change about Christianity if it wasn't true? Now read 1 Corinthians 15:1-28 and answer the question again.

3. We primarily focused on the intellectual and logical aspects of Jesus' death and resurrection. Re-read the passage I quoted from Titus above. How does Paul's description impact you emotionally?

---

[62] 1 Peter 3:18 (ESV)

[63] John 3:16 (NIV)

[64] Titus 3:3-7 (NIV)

10 THE RETURN

In case you haven't noticed, the story isn't over. Creation definitely hasn't been restored, and most people aren't living in a connected relationship with Him. His standards of love and justice aren't being carried out, and to put it bluntly, this world is massively screwed up. It's hard to believe God's ultimate plan was to get us to… this.

It wasn't. God's plan was and is complete restoration. And while He's given us a role in that restoration (which we'll discuss in the third section), we're not capable of pulling off all that He wants to accomplish. We need Him to come back. And that's another thing that all Christians who believe in the Resurrection and Revelation agree on. Jesus is coming back. Once again, we'll examine the pools of agreement before dipping our toes into the ocean of disagreement.

The first point of agreement is that Jesus will literally return. We've been waiting for it a long time, but the teaching is clear.

After the Resurrection, Jesus stuck around for a while, teaching His followers what they could expect, and what He expected from them. At the end of about forty days (a favorite God number), He took them to a mountainside (a favorite God place), gave them some final teaching, and left. Straight up into the clouds.

As soon as He got out of sight, the disciples were reminded He'd be coming back.

As they strained to see him rising into heaven, two white-robed men suddenly stood among them. "Men of Galilee," they said, "why are you standing here staring into heaven? Jesus has been taken from you into heaven, but someday he will return from heaven in the same way you saw him go!"[65]

That promise of a real return has shaped Christianity ever since. Paul, who wrote much of the New Testament, framed Jesus' return this way:

> *Behold! I tell you a mystery. We shall not all sleep, but we shall all be changed, in a moment, in the twinkling of an eye, at the last trumpet. For the trumpet will sound, and the dead will be raised imperishable, and we shall be changed. For this perishable body must put on the imperishable, and this mortal body must put on immortality.[66]*

He's coming back, and when He returns He's going to change us so we're like Him. Cool, huh?

But the Second Coming (as it's called) isn't just about us. It's also about God restoring His Kingdom to earth,[67] rewarding His followers,[68] judging those who continue to rebel against Him,[69] and bringing all creation back to the "very good" status it had in the beginning.

While we agree on these basics, Christians disagree strongly on the specifics. There are four prominent views on what we call The End Times, all with impressive names: Dispensational Premillennialism, Historical Premillennialism, Postmillennialism, and Realized Millennialism.

If you want to start an argument among Christians, this is an excellent topic to use. Many people who were raised in one view find it surprising there is real support for any other views. As Craig Keener puts it, "Every end-time view can seem reasonable if one has never sympathetically studied other views."[70]

Since the purpose of this section is to help you see the

---

[65] Acts 1:10-11 (NLT)

[66] 1 Corinthians 15:51-53 (ESV)

[67] Revelation 21:1-4

[68] 1 Corinthians 3:13-15

[69] Matthew 25:31-32

[70] *NIV Application Commentary: Revelation*, p. 25.

breadth of Christian faith, I'm not going to explain the four views, or encourage you to choose one. I'll save the descriptions for an appendix, where I'll also introduce you to my theory on why there is so much disagreement.[71]

Clarifying Heaven

Okay, you know how I said we'd be sticking to what everyone who commits to Revelation and Resurrection believes? I hope you don't mind if I break my own rule for a few paragraphs to clarify a few things about eternity and what happens after the "End Times." It seems to me a lot of Christians have really gotten confused in this area, and I think it will really help you write your faith in your own handwriting if you get this right, even if some Christians don't agree.

First, we don't believe in reincarnation, the idea that after we die we come back as someone or something else. We also don't believe in annihilation, that at death we simply cease to exist. We believe that God's people live forever with Him[72] after Jesus restores all things.

One huge misunderstanding some people have is understanding eternity as being a brand new thing. It isn't. Eternity (or Heaven, if you will) is a continuation of the story God's been telling since He spoke the world into existence. It's not God beginning a new story. To help us see this, the Bible contains one neat image that recurs throughout and helps tie the story together, right into eternity.

Early on, the Bible talks about the Garden of Eden, where Adam and Eve lived. It describes the rivers that flowed in Eden, as well as the trees that flourished there, bringing life to the inhabitants.[73] Later, in the book of Ezekiel, there is a foretelling of end times, and Ezekiel focuses on rivers and

---

[71] It's the second half of the "End Times" appendix.

[72] Since one of God's perfections is omnipresence, that He is present everywhere, this isn't really the limiting factor some assume.

[73] Genesis 2:8-10

healing trees.[74]

Then, in the last book of the Bible, Heaven is described:

Then the angel showed me a river with the water of life, clear as crystal, flowing from the throne of God and of the Lamb. It flowed down the center of the main street. On each side of the river grew a tree of life, bearing twelve crops of fruit, with a fresh crop each month. The leaves were used for medicine to heal the nations.[75]

The middle book in the Bible is the book of Psalms. It starts this way:

Blessed is the one
who does not walk in step with the wicked
or stand in the way that sinners take
or sit in the company of mockers,
but whose delight is in the law of the Lord,
and who meditates on his law day and night.
That person is like a tree planted by streams of water,
which yields its fruit in season
and whose leaf does not wither—
whatever they do prospers.[76]

A river and healing trees in the beginning of the story, the middle, and the end. So, Heaven isn't a new story. It's just the next chapter in the story God's been telling. And we're part of the story. Which brings us to something else people tend to get confused about when they talk about Heaven.

You've probably seen the pictures. Winged people in white robes, playing harps in the clouds. For many, that's what they think of when someone mentions Heaven.

Personally, that just sounds to me like a less-terrible Hell. For one thing, I'm afraid of heights, so floating in the clouds would be terrifying. Second, I don't like harp music. (And

---

[74] Ezekiel 47:1-12
[75] Revelation 22:1-2 (NLT)
[76] Psalm 1:1-3 (NIV)

don't know many people who do. Spotify doesn't even have a harp music option.) Finally, can you say BORING?

But because Heaven is a continuation of God's story, there is nothing in the Bible to suggest we'll have wings, live in clouds, or play harps. (Or even that most angels have wings.) It does suggest that we'll be continuing the purposes for which we were created: glorify God and manage His creation. Matter of fact, in the beginning of the Bible, the creation story says we were created to **rule** over creation.[77] At the very end of the Bible, it says we "will **reign** for ever and ever."[78] Eternity for us isn't just an eternal worship service. Instead, it's a time of purpose and activity as part of worship.

And as for the whole cloud thing, in eternity the point isn't that we go to Heaven. It's that Heaven will be here with us, in this physical universe, not in some ethereal spiritual realm.

Then I saw a new heaven and a new earth, for the old heaven and the old earth had disappeared. And the sea was also gone. And I saw the holy city, the new Jerusalem, coming down from God out of heaven like a bride beautifully dressed for her husband. I heard a loud shout from the throne, saying, "Look, God's home is now among his people! He will live with them, and they will be his people. God himself will be with them."[79]

In other words, as the continuation of God's story, Heaven is a home game. And if you wouldn't mind a little fun speculation, if we combine a couple of other truths we've already learned with what we see here, we might have an intriguing idea of what Heaven might be like.

On September 3, 2003, NASA pointed the Hubble Telescope at what looked like an empty, black part of space, then focused on that seemingly empty spot for four months. At the end of that time, they didn't discover a bunch of new

---

[77] Genesis 1:26
[78] Revelation 22:5 (NIV)
[79] Revelation 21:1-3 (NLT)

stars. They discovered a bunch of new galaxies, each containing billions of stars.[80]

Which makes me ask a question. Why did God make the universe so big? I used to say it was to help us appreciate how big and powerful He is. Which is true. But maybe there's an even deeper answer.

See, the universe is a revelation of God. There are things we can learn about God from creation we can't learn from anything else. And there are things I can learn about God in one place that I won't learn in another. The night sky over my house teaches me things about God that are different from what I learn watching a storm at the beach, or watching a sunset in the mountains. And even those change depending on which mountains or which beach or what time of year.

So, are there things I could learn about God on one of the moons of Jupiter that I can't learn on earth at all? And are there things I could learn in a valley of a planet circling one of the stars in one of those distant galaxies that I couldn't learn about our infinite God anywhere else in the universe? And could it be that another reason the universe is so big is that God is so awesome it takes a universe as big as ours, and an eternity of time,[81] to begin to learn everything God wants to teach us about Himself?

Just something to think about as we get back to the things we all agree on.

Practicing Your Penmanship

1. Unfortunately, our discussions about Jesus' Second Coming can be quite stale, detailed, and emotionless. However, one big purpose of the teaching is to inspire us as we live for Jesus. Can you think of some reasons why the idea that Jesus will return

---

[80] http://www.ba-bamail.com/content_12288/
Looking_At_the_Earth_With_True_Perspective.aspx
[81] If you really want to blow your mind on the concept of Heaven, remember that this universe isn't eternal. It will end in a few billion years, and God will then do something else to teach us about Himself.

and restore His creation should motivate us?

2. If you're part of a group that wants to take this conversation to another level, or if you just want to dig in more yourself, read and discuss/contemplate the appendix, What Jesus' First Coming Should Teach Us about His Second.

3. When you think of the concept of living eternally, what ideas do you find attractive? Unattractive? Scary? Challenging?

11 THE ANNOUNCEMENT
AND A REMINDER

It's good to be reminded of certain things. Jesus knew that, so He instituted a couple of events we call sacraments,[82] ceremonies we are instructed to perform until Jesus comes back.

The first of these is baptism. Baptism, at its heart, is an announcement. When people first came to accept Jesus, they were baptized to announce that decision. Now the methods of baptism vary greatly. Some baptize infants to announce they will be raised to follow Jesus. Some baptize immediately after conversion, some have a teaching process prior to the act. Some baptize by sprinkling or pouring water over the person, some immerse completely. Some groups even argue over whether to immerse three times forward or one time backwards. But despite the disagreements over form, the act itself is universal in Christendom, and whenever a person makes the decision to become a Christ follower, baptism is the announcement sacrament.

At our church, we baptize anyone who is old enough to make their own decision to follow Jesus, and do dedication services for infants instead of baptisms. We baptize by immersion because we believe that best reflects what the word baptize means, and also because baptism is meant to symbolize us dying to ourselves and rising to a new life in

---

[82] Two sacraments are universally accepted, but other groups or denominations have additional sacraments. Because the others are not universal, I'm not going to discuss them here. Some, like marriage for Roman Catholics, are accepted by nearly everyone but not considered sacraments. Others, like foot washing for some Christians, aren't universally accepted as actions we should all still be doing.

Jesus. We believe immersion best pictures the symbol. Plenty of good Christians do it differently, but again, they all do baptisms.

The second sacrament is Communion, also known as the Lord's Supper or the Eucharist. Jesus instructed us to commemorate and in some sense reenact His last meal with His closest followers before the Crucifixion. Again, observing Communion is universal, as are the two basic elements, wine and bread. But the methodology is incredibly diverse, as is the understanding of the act.

For some, Jesus is literally present in the wine and bread. For others, it is purely symbolic, and for others it is "powerfully symbolic," with Jesus or the Holy Spirit present in the actions, but not the elements.

As for the elements themselves, Roman Catholics only use unleavened bread (bread made without yeast) for their Eucharist. Eastern Orthodox only use leavened bread for theirs. Protestants pick and choose. Some groups use wine, some use grape juice.[83] Some use a common cup, some small, individual cups. Some tear pieces off of a loaf, some distribute wafers. Finally, some groups observe (or celebrate) Communion at every worship service, some only once or twice a year.

The bottom line is that we all believe we are supposed to observe this sacrament regularly to remind ourselves of the meaning of His death.[84] Every time we take the bread which reminds us of His body, we remember it was broken for us. Every time we drink from the cup, we are reminded of His blood which was shed for us. In a very minor way, we participate in all He went through, and are motivated to continue to follow Him.

And the part we agree on is much more important than the parts we don't.

---

[83] Which Thomas Bramwell Welch developed specifically so churches could do communion alcohol free. Really.

[84] 1 Corinthians 11:23-26

Actually, I hope you've seen that we agree on a lot of important things, even while leaving a lot of room for personal interpretation.

Some people might think I'm just making all this up, or that my list what all the people who believe in Revelation and Resurrection agree on is my personal, arbitrary list.

Well, as I was writing this chapter, I was also reading a fascinating book called *The Lost History of Christianity*, by John Philip Jenkins. He writes about a church leader named Timothy who lived a couple hundred years before what is now the Eastern Orthodox Church and the Roman Catholic Church split, and about five hundred years before the Protestant Reformation. In Timothy's day there were three primary groups of Christians, divided primarily by the details with which they understood Jesus' status as both God and man.

Around A.D. 800, Timothy compiled a list of the things that all three agreed upon. "… all shared a faith in the Trinity, the Incarnation, baptism, adoration of the Cross, the holy Eucharist, the two Testaments; all believed in the resurrection of the dead, eternal life, the return of Christ in glory, and the last judgment."[85]

Which sounds an awful lot like our list, and a lot of other lists you'll find, so I think we're on pretty solid ground in what we define as essential.

But I don't want to give the impression that the areas of disagreement are unimportant or inconsequential. These distinctions define our individual churches and denominations, and I think they also help us do a better job spreading the Good News.

The distinctions mean that people who are most drawn to transcendent worship have churches that focus on the otherness of God, while those who are naturally drawn to immanent worship have churches that help them feel God is near.

---

[85] Location 81 in Kindle version.

And don't think the doctrinal disputes are unimportant. In most cases, some churches are right and some are wrong. It's just that we can't let secondary disputes rise to the level of importance of the defining teachings like the Resurrection and the Deity of Christ, and certainty in these secondary areas is hard to come by.

If you are already connected to a church, it would be a good idea to find out about your church's distinctives. And if you are reading this book as part of a church study, this would be a good time to have someone explain why your church holds to its distinctives.

If you are not connected to a church and want some guidance on choosing, I'd like for you to finish the book before discussing it. For that reason, I'm saving "Choosing a Church" for the end.

Now, with these foundational truths in place, we should be ready to move on to section that gives the book its name, helping you write your faith in your own handwriting.

Practicing Your Penmanship

1. If you are part of a church, or are reading this book with a church group, this would be an excellent time to get someone from the church to explain the church's doctrinal distinctives.

2. Why does your church believe these more specific teachings? What Bible passages do they use to support these teachings?

3. How do you think these distinctives impact the church's mission and strategy? What advantages does your church gain because of these specific teachings?

4. Which of the distinctives do you find most attractive? Which are the most challenging?

Part 3:
Your Faith

12 WRITING YOUR FAITH

One of the things I love about the Bible is its humanity. We talk a lot about its inspiration, that

"No prophecy was ever produced by the will of man, but men spoke from God as they were carried along by the Holy Spirit."[86]

But often we forget to talk about the men themselves.[87] Even though they are being moved by God, their personalities shine through. Mark seemed to always be in a hurry. John wrote with a compassion that belied his nickname as a Son of Thunder.[88] And Paul. Well, with Paul we actually get to watch him grow in his faith.

His first appearances in the Bible display his natural impulsiveness and passion. He was quick to act, slow to forgive, always decisive. As he aged and matured, he mellowed. His passion remained, but he became wiser, forgave more readily, showed much more patience and understanding.

A great example is the way Paul treated Mark.[89] Mark accompanied Paul and Barnabas on their very first mission trip, but for some reason he abandoned the team.[90] When Paul and Barnabas were getting ready to take their next trip, Barnabas, who was a man of second chances, wanted to bring Mark along again. Paul disagreed so strongly that he wouldn't

---

[86] 2 Peter 1:21 (ESV)

[87] As far as we know, all the books of the Bible were written by men. If that turns out not to be the case, we can change the gender tags here.

[88] Mark 3:17

[89] Mark is frequently also called John Mark, and sometimes just John.

[90] Acts 13:13

even travel with Barnabas anymore.[91] But later in life, we see Paul encouraging others to trust Mark,[92] and finally even admitting how helpful he had become.[93]

Throughout Paul's life, we see God sanding off the rough edges and helping Paul become the person God created him to be. But his personality was refined, not removed. Paul was a unique creation when God started working on him, and God's work only served to enhance the uniqueness, not eliminate it.

In the books of the Bible Paul wrote, we see his handwriting getting more mature but also more distinct. We see Paul's faith, written in his own unique handwriting, not bending to become just like every other Biblical writer.

And that's what God wants to do with you. Not turn you into a clone, but refine your uniqueness so you can be the best possible you, the person He created you to be.

As we've said from the beginning, God wants you to write your faith in your own handwriting. But how is that accomplished?

Well, the transformation involves a few key tools that God uses in the process. They include the Bible, prayer, and commitment. Through the rest of the book, we'll look at those tools, how we cooperate with God in the process, and how God uses them to help you write your unique faith in your own handwriting.

Before we get to the tools, I probably should introduce you to your partner.

---

[91] Acts 15:37-40
[92] Colossians 4:10
[93] 2 Timothy 4:11

13 THE HANDWRITING PARTNERSHIP

Lots of people try to write their faith in their own handwriting and end up with a scribbled mess. The challenge is that Christian faith isn't a solo undertaking, and it's definitely not a purely "me" endeavor.

When it comes to developing your faith, you have a very important partner, a partner uniquely gifted to helping you become the distinctive person God created you to be.

In Philippians chapter 2 we find a couple of interesting verses.

> *"Therefore, my dear friends, as you have always obeyed ... continue to work out your salvation with fear and trembling, for it is God who works in you to will and to act in order to fulfill his good purpose."*[94]

If you read closely, you'll see Paul (the author) comes awfully close to contradicting himself. First, he says to work hard on your faith. *Work out your salvation with fear and trembling.* But then he says that God is the one doing the work: *for it is God who works in you to will and to act in order to fulfill his good purpose.*

While it sounds like a contradiction (I work it out but God does the work.), it's actually just a picture of the partnership that must emerge if we're going to write our faith in our own handwriting—at least if we want that faith to actually work.

See, God has a plan for you. People disagree about how detailed the plan is, but it has two components. The first part of the plan is that God wants you to be like Jesus. *God knew*

---

94 Philippians 2:12-13 (NIV)

his people in advance, and he chose them to become like his Son.[95] That "willing and acting" we saw in Philippians 2 is about you learning to think and act the way Jesus would in your situations. God accomplishes that from the inside out by changing the way your mind works. *Do not conform to the pattern of this world, but be transformed by the renewing of your mind.*[96]

The second component of the plan is that God has a purpose (or purposes) for you.

> *For we are God's masterpiece. He has created us anew in Christ Jesus, so we can do the good things he planned for us long ago.*[97]

God has a plan for His creation, and you are part of that plan.

Which points immediately to two problems. One, I'm still that fallen, selfish creature we've discussed all along. If I'm fully in charge of my own transformation, I'll either end up more selfish and fallen, or instead of modeling Jesus, I'll create my own God in my mind and try to become like my fictional creation, instead of who Jesus really is.

Second, if I'm supposed to be part of God's plan, it would help to have more details about that plan and how I fit in. Again, if I just make up the plan, it will play more into my selfishness than God's selfless plan to restore creation.

So, we need a partner, and it would be best if that partner was, well, God. And thankfully, God is our partner in this process. Now, if we go back to our discussion on the Trinity, you may have noticed that each member of the Trinity has specific roles. God the Father rules from Heaven. God the Son (Jesus) was God's physical presence on earth who died for our sins, and rose again to bring us new life. But if you remember, Jesus went back to God the Father shortly after the Resurrection.

---

[95] Romans 8:29 (NLT)
[96] Romans 12:2 (NIV)
[97] Ephesians 2:10 (NLT)

The reason for His return to Heaven was simple. As the physical member of the Trinity, He limited Himself to being in one place at a time. But Christians were going to be everywhere. So after leaving, God sent the Holy Spirit, the third member of the Trinity. In much the same way the first person of the Trinity is God the Father and the second member is God the Son, if you don't mind an unusual analogy, the Holy Spirit is like God the Mother.

Seriously. Christians are born of the Spirit,[98] and the Spirit is in charge of raising us. He dwells in us,[99] cleans us up,[100] leads us to God's truths,[101] and works in our lives so we begin to think and act like Jesus.[102] Sounds like an awfully good Mother to me. And an excellent partner.

Now that we've established our partner in this process, and what some of His roles are, we can begin looking at the process God uses, and our role within that process.

Practicing Your Penmanship

1. Does it make you feel better or worse that God wants to work with you in developing your faith? Why?

2. If you were totally in charge of creating your own faith, how do you think it would differ from what God would want? How do you think it would be the same?

3. Okay, the concept the Holy Spirit being "God the Mother" is a bit odd. Can you think of ways it could be helpful? Are there ways you think it could keep us from the best possible view of God's Spirit?

---

[98] John 4:29 (TLB)
[99] Acts 13:52, Romans 8:9; 1 Corinthians 6:19
[100] Titus 3:5-6
[101] John 16:13
[102] Galatians 5:22-23

14 THE GROWTH CYCLE

Repetition is a form of emphasis.

Let me say that again. Repetition is a form of emphasis.

Jesus was giving his followers some final instructions prior to His death and resurrection. Some of the instructions were confusing for them, but that's to be understood. He was teaching them something brand new, something beyond what they'd been taught, something they would never have considered on their own.

He said it first in John 14:15-17:

If you love me, obey my commandments. And I will ask the Father, and he will give you another Advocate, who will never leave you. He is the Holy Spirit, who leads into all truth. The world cannot receive him, because it isn't looking for him and doesn't recognize him. But you know him, because he lives with you now and later will be in you.[103]

In case they missed it, He repeated the same basic thing in slightly different words in verse 21:

Those who accept my commandments and obey them are the ones who love me. And because they love me, my Father will love them. And I will love them and reveal myself to each of them.[104]

Then to underline it, write it in caps, and boldface the type, He said it one more time only two verses later:

All who love me will do what I say. My Father will love them,

---

[103] John 14:15-17 (NLT)
[104] John 14:21 (NLT)

and we will come and make our home with each of them.[105]

Repetition is a form of emphasis. Jesus is definitely wanting to emphasize something, and I believe what He is emphasizing is the key to cooperating with the Holy Spirit to write our faith in our own handwriting. It's a three-step process that I call The Growth Cycle. It's really clear in verse 21:

> *Those who accept my commandments and obey them are the ones who love me. And because they love me, my Father will love them. And I will love them and reveal myself to each of them.*[106]

Step One: Obedience shows love. In this step, the Holy Spirit reveals a truth about God[107] that is not true about us. For example, God's Spirit may show us that God is forgiving, but we have been holding a grudge.

We then have a choice to make. Do we continue living in opposition to God's nature, or do we adjust our lives to be more like Him?

If we choose to make the adjustment, to obey God by living into His standard of forgiveness, God does something amazing. He sees past our action to the underlying attitude. He chooses to see in it the seeds of love, and interprets the action as love. We may not think of it that way, but whenever God sees us moving towards His standards, He calls it obedience, and interprets it as love.

Step Two: Love is rewarded with revelation. Next, God looks at our obedience, interprets it as love, and chooses to reward it. But the reward isn't what you might expect. He doesn't give us more stuff or make our lives easier. That's nothing. He gives us the greatest gift possible. Since He's the greatest Being imaginable, He gives us more of Himself. Or, more specifically, He reveals more of Himself to us. Which

---

[105] John 14:23 (NLT)
[106] John 14:21 (NLT)
[107] *When the Spirit of truth comes, he will guide you into all truth.* John 16:13a (NLT)

leads to Step Three.

Step Three: Greater revelation calls for greater obedience. That reward comes with a challenge. As we see God more clearly, we recognize another area where something that is true of God isn't true of us. And we're confronted with the same choice. Do we obey, moving our lives closer to God's standards, or not?

Now, here's the cool part. If we choose to obey, to move our lives once again closer to God's standards, we start the cycle all over again. Greater obedience proves greater love, which is rewarded with an even greater revelation of God, which leads to even greater obedience, and the cycle just keeps going.

And here's the even cooler part. It doesn't matter how much faith we have, how great the obedience, or how far along we are on our faith journey. God sees our obedience as love and rewards it by revealing more about Himself.

It could be that you're just curious about Jesus and choose to learn more by attending church or reading the Bible or even asking a Christian friend some questions. God sees that movement toward Him as obedience and a microscopic form of love, so He rewards it with more truth.

You may have just decided to accept what Jesus did for you and become His follower. God then says the first step of that faith is to obey by being baptized. And if we obey, we continue the cycle.

You can be a lifetime follower who has been taught amazing truths and done amazing things for God. Every obedience leads God to show you even more of Himself and take you to even deeper obedience.

And because God's goal is for you to be just like Jesus, and because all of us still have a long way to go, the cycle works no matter how far you are from God, or how close. It works to get things started for the person who is farthest from God, it keeps things going for the most mature follower.

Discontinuing the cycle is also the easiest way to halt our

growth. We just have to stop obeying. We decide not to do something we know God wants us to do. It could be a negative action God wants us to stop or a positive action God wants us to start. If we say No, in the same way obedience keeps the cycle going, disobedience stops it.

Of course, the cycle gives us the way to get progress going again. If you've stalled, ask God to show you one way you're not living like He wants you to live. Do what He reveals, and the cycle resumes.

Want to know the greatest thing about this process? It is completely personalized.

A lot of times when people begin following Jesus, they are given a template. "Here's what it looks like to be a Christian." That's why the members of so many churches all tend to look and act alike. Rather than allow the admittedly dangerous process of letting the Holy Spirit work in the life of each individual, new believers are given a list of do's and don'ts, or trained in the proper attitudes and actions of believers, or some other method of producing Christian clones.

That's not how Jesus did it when He was on earth. Peter was loud and outspoken from the day he met Jesus until his last appearance in the Bible. John, on the other hand, went from a "Son of Thunder"[108] to someone who liked to lean in close and love people.[109] Paul tended to be quiet in person,[110] until he was provoked into obnoxiousness, either verbal[111] or written, though as we mentioned, we can watch as God mellows him with time.[112]

From my experience, the Holy Spirit doesn't seem that interested in producing clones today. He wants to transform each of us into masterpieces,[113] and the only way to do this is not with paint-by-numbers discipleship, but rather by placing

---

[108] Mark 3:17

[109] John 21:20

[110] 2 Corinthians 10:10

[111] Galatians 2:14

[112] Acts 15:37-39; Colossians 4:10; 2 Timothy 4:11

[113] Ephesians 2:10 (NLT)

the Holy Spirit inside each of us, letting Him show us how He wants to transform us, and encouraging us to cooperate in the process.

Now, before you get too excited, there are a few downsides.

For one, this process goes against our nature. Our primary responsibility in this is obedience, and we all hate obeying.

But obedience is the centerpiece. That's why, in the verses we started with from Philippians, the first words weren't about deep spiritual truths. They were about obedience:

"Therefore, my dear friends, as you have always **obeyed**...[114]

Another downside is that God may not change you the way you want Him to. You know your failings, and you probably have things you want Him to change first. He will probably chose a different order, and then use methods you're not that crazy about.

Also, when other people look at you, they will identify what areas of your life they think need changing—and they'll want God to start His work in those areas. Then, when God chooses to work on something else first, some good people may be disappointed or even angry with you because you're not following their program.

Finally, this is a messy, uncontrollable method. Speaking as a pastor, the idea of letting each person grow as God wants them to can be terrifying. Control can be much more comfortable.

The upside for churches is that if we let Him, God can create an army of uniquely gifted and trained people who are ready to advance God's Kingdom His way. And as individuals we get to be the unique masterpieces God created us to be. We get to live a life with real meaning. And we get the joy that only comes from being connected to God, living in His will, and seeing Him change the world through us.

If you don't like this messy method, there are plenty of

---

[114] Philippians 2:12-13 (NIV)

cookie-cutter opportunities out there to help you look just like one group of Christians or another. Personally, I prefer the messy method. If you do, too, let's keep going.

Which, of course, leads to a crucial question: If the process starts with God revealing truths about Himself, how does He teach me these new truths? How do I know His purpose in my life? How do I know my next step? Well, that's our next chapter.

Practicing Your Penmanship

1. Given the choice, would you prefer an individualized growth process or a cookie-cutter system? What advantages do you see in both? Does this system scare you any? Why?

2. How uncomfortable are you with the idea that the key to spiritual maturity is obedience? Would you have hoped it was something else? What might you have preferred? Can you see any benefits to building your faith on obedience?

3. Is there something you know God wants you to do that you've been putting off? Do you think it is hindering your spiritual development?

15 TRUTH REVEALED

It was the summer between my junior and senior years of college. My dad was just beginning that Sunday morning's sermon, reading from Matthew 6. I'm not sure which verse he started with, or where he stopped. I know he read the first part of verse 33, but I can't honestly say I heard the second half. Because when he read, "But seek ye first the kingdom of God, and his righteousness;"[115] my life changed. God revealed a truth to me, I obeyed, and nothing was ever the same.

We've discussed the importance of obeying when God reveals truth to us, but left open the question of how God does the revealing. How can we best position ourselves to hear truth, and how do we know it is God speaking?

To answer that question, we need to look at the three places where God is most likely to speak to us.

Where to Listen: The Big Room

First, the really good news. God wants us to know His will more than we want to know it. Because of our screwed-up nature, we tend to move away from God's truth, so it's more a case of God pursuing us than us pursuing Him.

But why does it seem so difficult? Because we want Him to say what we want to hear, not what He wants to say. That's why it's crucial that the first place we start listening is a place we don't have much control over what we hear.

It's called church.

Now, I hear what some people are saying. With all the talk about the Bible earlier, shouldn't that be where we start?

---

[115] Matthew 6:33a (KJV)

Well, yes and no. I'm all for Bible reading, and I think a person who is interested in God should start reading the Bible immediately if not sooner. We'll talk about how to read the Bible in some detail later (our third place to listen). But the best place to start listening to what God wants to say to you through the Bible is to listen to a trained, gifted teacher.

I know I'm bucking the trend here. There are tons of people saying that the key to spiritual development is personal Bible study, even going so far as to say that you can't be a mature Christian without reading your Bible. I used to be one of those people. Then I realized something. If that was true it meant there were hardly any mature Christians for the first fifteen hundred years of the church.

See, prior to Guttenberg, people didn't own Bibles. Churches did.

The way people heard truths about God was they gathered together, and a trained teacher taught them. This has some serious advantages over just handing someone a Bible and saying, "Go."

For one, a trained teacher knows where the Bible keeps its landmines. Almost every heresy in history got its start by someone misreading the Bible, and much of the misreading comes about because the reader doesn't know the whole story. A trained teacher should know the whole Bible, a fair amount of church history, and a good deal of theology. That means the landmines get avoided, and these large-group teaching sessions provide a relatively safe place for God to speak.

Ideally, large-group teaching involves three conversations. First, the speaker is conversing with God. As a pastor and teacher, I spend the week talking to God, trying to discern what He wants me to teach, and how to best present it. This conversation continues all the way up to, and even into, the sermon. During the sermon, I'm trying to listen for any course corrections He wants to make and any information He wants me to share with that specific audience. Hopefully, I hear well enough to facilitate the next two conversations.

The second conversation is between the teacher and the audience. Obviously, the teacher is talking to the audience, but the audience in most cases is also communicating back.[116] I know when I'm teaching the expressions on the faces, the stories I know about the people in the room, even the general mood of the room shape the direction of the message.

Then, if things are going well in the first two conversations, a third conversation can be triggered, a conversation between the listener and God.

That's what happened when I heard my dad read Matthew 6:33. He read it and the Holy Spirit said (not out loud), "Are you paying attention?" The way I sometimes describe it, the Spirit grabbed me by the shirt collar, drug my face down to the Bible, and wouldn't let me think about anything else until I'd dealt with that verse. "Seek first his kingdom and his righteousness." I memorized it, spent the rest of the day meditating on it, and basically never got it out of my system. When I got back to college that fall, the primary question people asked was, "What happened to Steve?"

God communicated a truth to me, I chose to obey by adjusting my life toward that truth, and God rewarded my obedience with transformation. While it's not usually that dramatic, the same thing should play out every time people gather to be taught the Bible. At our church, we stress that everyone should listen for the truth God wants them to hear, and take a step of obedience toward God in response.

My story may sound extreme, but one thing I've noticed throughout the years is how many people have a similar story. A time they were in church, the pastor said something, and BAM! Everything changed. So, when you're wanting to hear truths that God can use to help you write your faith in your

---

[116] I know there are plenty of video venues being used, and I'm all for them. We use video venues ourselves. One of the few negatives about video teaching is that, when it comes to this second conversation, the teacher has to assume the audience being addressed during the recording is characteristic of the audiences that will watch the video.

own handwriting, don't ignore the place where He's been doing it for two thousand years. The church.[117]

Where to Listen: The Small Room

There are problems with the big room, however. For one, there is little accountability. No one knows if I was really paying attention, whether or not I heard a truth I need to apply, or whether I followed through on my commitment to apply it.

That's where small group studies come in.

At our church they're called Connection Groups, but they go by many different names, from Sunday School to Faith Groups to Small Groups to, well, whatever catchy name a church may have come up with to make the whole idea more attractive.

People tend to avoid small groups, whatever they're called. The idea of other people knowing our business makes us uncomfortable. But they provide a necessary step between large group learning and personal Bible Study.

Here are some quick reasons you probably should include small-group study as you are listening for God to reveal truth in your life:

First, a small group gives you the opportunity for personalized voices to speak into your life. The pastor can say, "Love your neighbor." A friend in a small group can say, "Maybe you could go talk to the family that just moved in next door."

Small groups are also much better for accountability. "Did you talk to that new neighbor yet?" Plus they can provide support and encouragement when the step you need to take is more difficult than welcoming someone to the neighborhood. There are times in our lives we all need a hug, and other times we need a kick in the pants. Small groups allow us to make friends who know us well enough to know

---

117 Hebrews 10:25

which we need, and when.

Finally, small groups can function like training wheels. As we start trying to understand the Bible for ourselves, we sometimes make some colossal errors. (Where do you think all those cults come from?) A small group is a place where we can say, "I think that passage means…", knowing if we're totally off base someone can tell us before we do something crazy.

To put it another way, why do we need to hear the Bible taught in a large-group setting by trained teachers, and in small-group settings with a few friends? Three words: Westboro Baptist Church. When we isolate ourselves from trained teachers, we can make the Bible say anything we want it to. And if we don't have friends who are also learning the Bible with us (some of whom know more than we do), there's no one to tell us we're being idiots. Next thing you know, we're picketing military funerals and giving the Church a major PR problem.

Of course, you probably won't go that weird. But all of us tend toward extremes. Some people tend toward judgmentalism, where everyone but me is wrong and needs zapping, while others lean toward the idea that whatever anyone wants to do is okay as long as they're sincere. Some of us tend toward helping people without telling them about Jesus, while others want to tell people about Jesus without helping meet their needs.

If you don't mind a twisted analogy, the Road of Faith is surrounded by The Ditches of Stupidity. (That should have been in *The Princess Bride*.) Large and small groups are like the guardrails that keep us out of those ditches, and help make sure we can get the most out of the third place we should listen for His voice, personal Bible study.

And that's such a big topic, it gets its own chapter.

Practicing Your Penmanship

1. Do you currently have a church you consider "yours?" What is something you have learned recently from the large-room teaching there? (If you don't attend a church, check out the appendix, "Choosing a Church.")

2. Have you ever heard someone teaching something you know is wrong? Did that mistaken teaching lead to any damaging actions, either for the people who taught it, or for the way people view God or the church? (Feel free to rant about Westboro Baptist Church, but try to come up with other examples as well.)

3. Do you find the idea of a small group attractive or off-putting? What challenges would you have to overcome to regularly be part of one? Have you ever had any negative experiences as part of a group? Positive experiences? What do you think is the greatest value of meeting with a small group?

16 THE PRIVATE ROOM

Hello, my name is Steve, and I'm a Bible junkie.

I've spent my life studying it, and I'm still finding amazing things.

But to get the right stuff out of the Bible, I have to read it properly. That means understanding some things about it, some things about me, and some techniques to help read it accurately.

Let's start with a spectacular truth the Bible reveals about itself.

> *All Scripture is inspired by God and is useful to teach us what is true and to make us realize what is wrong in our lives. It corrects us when we are wrong and teaches us to do what is right. God uses it to prepare and equip his people to do every good work.[118]*

Then a little something about its origin:

> *Above all, you must understand that no prophecy of Scripture came about by the prophet's own interpretation of things. For prophecy never had its origin in the human will, but prophets, though human, spoke from God as they were carried along by the Holy Spirit.[119]*

And finally, let's throw in a truth about it many people have never considered:

> *Jesus performed many other signs in the presence of his disciples, which are not recorded in this book. But these are written that you may believe that Jesus is the Messiah, the Son of God, and*

---

[118] 2 Timothy 3:16-17 (NLT)
[119] 2 Peter 1:20-21 (NIV)

that by believing you may have life in his name.[120]

Put them together and what do we have? God inspired the writing of the Bible, moving the human authors along by the Holy Spirit, with the intention of revealing God to us in order to equip us to become who He wants us to be and do what He wants us to do. This purpose extends all the way to what stories were included and which were excluded. With every passage in the Bible, we can ask the questions why is this in the Bible, and how can it impact the way I live my life?

Toward the end of this section, we'll even see how this can apply to a passage you would never dream could be relevant to your life.

Read It

Let's say you've never read *To Kill a Mockingbird*, even though you've heard for years what a great book it is. Finally you give in, pick up a copy, and begin. First, you flip over to page 75 and read a chapter. Then, you move about two-thirds of the way through the book and read a page or two, then read the book's last three pages and the first two. For the next few weeks, you continue the process, sometimes reading a paragraph from the middle of a chapter, sometimes re-reading sections. At the end of two months, you've read the first chapter three or four times, the last page twice, most of part one, hardly any of part two.

Ready to give your book report?

Well, that's how most people read the Bible. Even worse, that's how a lot of people read each of the 66 individual books that make up the Bible. Psalms and Matthew? Read them—or at least parts of them. Zephaniah, Lamentations, and Philemon? Are those even in there? (They are.)

Here's the deal. The Bible is one book telling one story, but using 66 books written by dozens of people over centuries of time to tell it. When we choose to ignore entire

---

[120] John 20:30-31 (NIV)

sections of the book, we're missing pieces of the story. And since the Bible's purpose is to reveal God and transform us, we're missing out on vital truths about God and key changes God wants to make in our lives.

The good news? It's not that hard to read, and it's not *that* long. (The Harry Potter series is about 300,000 words longer than the Bible.) Granted, there are sections in the Bible that are hard to understand, and others that challenge our ability to focus. But the hard ones don't impact any major teaching, and (let's just go ahead and say it) the boring ones are balanced with some really exciting stuff.

More good news, unlike *To Kill a Mockingbird*, you don't have to read it completely in order. Just try to read each book as a whole instead of hunting and pecking around looking for nuggets of deep meaning. Matter of fact, I even created a reading plan to help first-timers get through the whole Bible in a year. It's got introductions to each book, and tries to balance the exciting and the boring to help you keep moving. You can download it from my website, pastorstevedavis.info.[121]

Study it.

So, you've read the Bible through, or at least enough to get a grasp of the overall picture. Now you want to start digging in. The best way to start is by asking the right questions. Here are a few I find incredibly helpful.

Why is this here? Remember that verse that said not everything Jesus did made it into the Bible, but only the stories that would encourage our spiritual growth?[122] One thing that means is that we can safely ask a seemingly impertinent question like this one. God put every passage in there for a reason, and that reason normally includes teaching

---

[121] The Bible App from YouVersion also has some great reading plans. They have one called "OWNit365 One Story" that gives a great overview of the whole Bible if you want to get to the next step more quickly.
[122] John 20:30-31

me more about God, showing me how to be more like Jesus, and advancing His story on earth. I have built entire small-group studies out of simply trying to answer this question. It can lead you to some great insights.

What is the genre? That may sound weird, but it's crucial. Those 66 books of the Bible cover a multitude of styles and genres. There are letters, poems, prophecies, historical narratives, and others. Trying to read a poem like a historical narrative, or a legal section like a letter can lead to some fascinating problems.

By the way, this is one of the reasons for the disagreements on God's method of creation. Are the first three chapters of Genesis poetry, like David's song of praise in 2 Samuel 22, where God is pictured as rescuing David like a dragon flying down from heaven, or historical narrative, like Moses' description of the construction of the high priest's garments in Exodus 28? The answer may seem obvious to you, but whatever you think, there are really good Christians who disagree.

Thankfully, for the overwhelming majority of the Bible, the genre question is settled. Romans is a letter, Job is wisdom poetry, and Revelation is a weird genre called apocalyptic. And if those words don't mean much to you, there is a great book called *How to Read the Bible for All Its Worth* by Gordon D. Fee and Douglas Stuart. It doesn't cost that much and can really help with these and other questions.

Here's another question that impacts how people understand the first few chapters of Genesis as well as every other passage in the Bible:

What was the original author's focus and intention? We already saw that the Bible was written intentionally. Well, what was the intention? In Genesis, was Moses trying to give us the universe's construction details, refute the teachings of the surrounding peoples in the region, point us to the magnificence of God, all of the above, or something else entirely? When Paul wrote the book of Romans, what questions was he trying to answer? What impact did the author of Job hope to have in the lives of his hearers? These questions can open the door to amazing insights as you study the Bible.

This question is tied closely to the next question to ask:

What did the original audience hear? Try to imagine living like the original hearers. You're sitting in a stone building in ancient Corinth. The Romans control everything. On a hill above the city sits a massive temple to Aphrodite that employs temple prostitutes (who possibly kept their heads shaved as a mark of their profession and well as their dedication.[123]) Around the corner is a temple to Caesar where you just might be asked to make an offering and say, "Caesar is Lord."

It was a very different world, and it really helps us to at least try to bridge the thought gap instead of pretending these pre-literate people thought just like modern Westerners. Sometimes, if we're not careful, we're asking questions they could never have conceived of. Sometimes we're trying to make them fit into our way of viewing the world using modern categories they would never have imagined.

Of course, we'll never be able to really get in their heads, but the introductions to the individual books found in many Bibles can help here. *How to Read the Bible Book by Book*, the sequel to *How to Read the Bible for All It's Worth*, can be a big help here as well. Even if you don't have those resources, there can be great value in making the effort to put ourselves in their sandals.

This kind of questioning can teach us wonderful things about the Bible as we look at it from different perspectives, much like looking at a sculpture from different angles often reveals new levels of beauty. Getting everything exactly right isn't the point (or even possible much of the time). Finding fresh insights from the new viewpoint is.

Now, before we start applying the Bible to our lives, let me give a couple warnings.

---

[123] Which could potentially impact how we understand 1 Corinthians 11:4-7.

First, God uses human speech forms to get across His truths and principles. That is a fact. The Bible contains historical statements, but it also contains hyperbole, poetry, even sarcasm. Some people say the Bible means what it says. Well, to be technical, it means what it means. Treating poetic statements like historical narratives can lead to some ridiculous concepts, like God breathing fire like a dragon.[124]

Second, my level of comfort with the meaning God intended is irrelevant. Some people may have trouble accepting that God uses sarcasm in the Bible. But Paul is certainly being sarcastic in Galatians 5:12,[125] and Job has one of the great sarcastic lines of all time. "You people really know everything, don't you? And when you die, wisdom will die with you!"[126]

Also, many people have trouble with the idea that the Bible uses exaggeration, but almost every follower of Jesus treats certain texts as hyperbole. For instance, some people don't want to admit that Jesus was using hyperbole when He said, "If your eye causes you to stumble, gouge it out and throw it away." However, I've never met a man who doesn't have trouble with his eyes causing him to stumble, at least occasionally, yet I've never seen a church full of one-eyed men.

If God wants to use hyperbole and poetry and sarcasm, well, He's God. He can do whatever He wants. My job is to adjust to Him, not try to get Him to adjust to my communication preferences.

Okay, rant over. Let's get to application.

Apply it.

Finally, the fun part. Taking what we're learning and applying it in our lives. Proper application takes three steps,

---

[124] 2 Samuel 22:9

[125] *As for those agitators, I wish they would go the whole way and emasculate themselves!* Galatians 5:12 (NIV)

[126] Job 12:2 (NLT)

and they have to be done in order.

Step One: What it says. On the surface, what does the text say? David slings a stone and the giant crashes to the ground.[127] A healthy fear of God is the beginning of wisdom.[128] Don't commit murder or steal.[129]

This is usually a simple step, but always crucial. If we detach our personal application from what the text actually says, we've detached it from its source. We can make it say anything and mean nothing.

A more pertinent example: The Bible says twice that there is no God. Of course, both times it prefaces the statement by telling us, "The fool says in his heart, 'There is no God.'"[130] What the text says is that a person who denies the existence of God is a fool in the big-picture sense, no matter how smart they are in other areas of life.

And here's the rule. A given text only says one thing. David fired off that rock, not his brother, not King Saul, and not some symbolic force. David did it. Our study may provide greater details into what the text says, but it still only says one thing.

Step Two: What it means. What general principles does this passage teach about God, how He works, and what He wants from people?

This gets a little more subjective, but only a little. While each text only says one thing, it can mean more than one. In the story of David and Goliath, what it says is a description of a specific battle. What it means includes that God is in control of every battle. That it doesn't matter how big the enemy is, God is bigger. That God rewards faith that is willing to risk. There is a list of principles the passage teaches, but it is a finite list. It doesn't mean that if we take risks for

---

[127] 1 Samuel 17

[128] Proverbs 9:10

[129] Exodus 20:13, 15

[130] Psalm 14:1 and 53:1

God we'll always win because that separates us from what the rest of the Bible teaches us.[131] It doesn't mean that God likes short people or doesn't like tall people, because the text makes it clear that the point is about the combatants' relationship with and attitude toward God, not their heights.

Here's where it can get both fun and challenging. For some passages, finding those principles can be difficult, especially when we're dealing with really different cultures. This is where we have to start translating. Not translating from one language to another, but from one culture to another.

A great example of translating was done in the 18th and 19th Centuries. There are a lot of Bible passages that talk about how to treat slaves, but none that even hint that we should try to abolish slavery. Yet Christians were the ones who led the charge to end slavery in both Britain and the United States, and Christians are still on the front lines fighting human trafficking worldwide. How did we get from rules about slavery to its abolition? Translation.

See, when Paul wrote his letters, slavery was an entrenched social institution and there was nothing the handful of Christians in the Roman world could do about it. So Paul gave principles on how to operate in a culture where slavery was legal and even normal. But sixteen hundred years later, believers who had positions of power took a look at those same admonitions and recognized an underlying principle. All people, even slaves, are made in the image of God. They also realized that one application of those principles was that one image of God shouldn't mistreat another one, and probably shouldn't own one to begin with. They concluded that if Christians had the power to do something about a practice that defamed the image of God in people, they should. So they did.

Jesus also did some interesting translation work with the Ten Commandments. He took two commandments, Don't murder and Don't commit adultery, and combined them with the principles found in the second half of the Ten Commandments (the part focused on humans). In the same way that we shouldn't covet because it is the root sin behind stealing, we shouldn't hate or lust, because those are the roots of murder[132] and adultery.[133]

Obviously, translation can be challenging or even dangerous. My tendency is to ignore what the text says, or to force the text to mean what I want it to mean. But it's also helpful because when done properly we can learn some important things, and grow to be like Jesus in ways we hadn't considered.

Or at least, that's what can happen when we finally get to the third step.

Step Three: What it means to me. Finally, the good part. Application. We know what it says. We know what it means. Now I can ask what it means to me.

This is where the Holy Spirit steps to the forefront because He helps us turn principles into life change. It goes like this. I'm reading the story of David and Goliath. I see what it says. (Victorious teen, dead giant.) I recognize what it means, the principles that underlie the text. Then, as I think about it (the religious word is meditating), the Spirit points out a specific area of my life where one of the principles intersects my reality.

For instance, say I have a friend who has a powerful enemy where she works. She worries that this person is going to manipulate things so she'll lose her job. But the morning before a big meeting, she reads 1 Samuel 17, David and Goliath. As she reads, she understands what the text says, then thinks about the one of the meanings of the passage: God is bigger than any giant. At this point the Holy Spirit plants a thought in her mind: *God is bigger than any giant,*

---

132 Matthew 5:21-26
133 Matthew 5:27-28

including that person at work. Cue the feeling of comfort and confidence that come from being reminded that God is in control of my situations.

Or I'm reading Galatians chapter 5, and come across, *"But the Holy Spirit produces this kind of fruit in our lives: love, joy, peace, patience, kindness ..."*[134] The Holy Spirit reminds me that my behavior toward one of my friends has been anything but kind. I then choose to obey by being kind, and... hey, we're back to the growth cycle!

Yep, it all ties together. Properly reading the Bible is one of the most crucial ways that God can communicate personal truth into our lives so the growth cycle can keep moving.

Journaling

One way to maximize the impact of your personal study is to write down what you learn.

The process is simple but powerful.

It's based on the method we just described, with a couple minor modifications. Before you start reading, ask God what He wants to teach you today. (By the way, that's a good habit even if you're not going to journal.)

Then as you read, try to be sensitive to the Holy Spirit's prompting on what He wants you to focus on that day. It could be a phrase that seems to jump off the page at you, or a verse that smacks right into your present situation, or even a word or two that you can't seem to make fit with what's around them.

Next open your journal (paper or electronic), and write down the verse or phrase and why you think it's important. Let your mind untangle the text as you pray and write, and don't be surprised if God reveals more to you during the writing process. Finally, write a prayer expressing how you're going to live out what you've learned. (Remember the obedience part of the growth cycle?)

---

[134] Galatians 5:22 (NLT)

As you read the Bible and write down what you learn, over time God will be able to teach you even more about Himself—and yourself. And don't forget to go back over your journal entries from time to time. You'll be amazed at the lessons you've learned and how He's used that information to help you grow.

One More Thing

As we'll see in the next chapter, prayer is also crucial for writing out our faith, but before we get to that I think I promised you we'd look at a passage you'd never dream could be relevant.

It's actually just three verses long, but it's a doozy. It's in one of the legal sections of the Bible, when God was giving the Israelites instructions on how to live while they traveled from Egypt to their promised land in what is now Israel.

Designate a place outside the camp where you can go to relieve yourself. As part of your equipment have something to dig with, and when you relieve yourself, dig a hole and cover up your excrement. For the LORD your God moves about in your camp to protect you and to deliver your enemies to you. Your camp must be holy, so that he will not see among you anything indecent and turn away from you.[135]

Told you it was a doozy, and at first glance it seems hard to see how instructions on burying feces could be relevant in a world of flush toilets. But let's first look at what it says. Sure, it says to take a spade to the bathroom (along with a magazine, I suppose). But it also tells them why. God is present in the camp to protect them, and you don't want to offend Him (which free-range poop would no doubt do).

So, what in the world does it mean? What are the principles underlying the feces-disposal manifesto?

Well, how about this? God is present with us. That's kind of cool. Also, God is holy. That's why they were to keep the

---

[135] Deuteronomy 23:12-14 (NIV)

place clean. Cleanliness is next to godliness isn't in the Bible, but this passage seems to imply it. Now, if you remember earlier, one of the things we learned about God is that He is both immanent (present with us) and transcendent (different from and above us). This interesting passage doesn't really teach those contrasting truths, but it does reflect them both. And the final principle, the one that sums up the whole thing, is that we are to look at every area of life, including the most mundane and private, and live in the awareness that God is both present in that situation and holy above it.

And what does that mean to me? How about, if the most mundane and private (and even a little disgusting) areas of my life are supposed to reflect God's immanence and transcendence, is there any area of my life that isn't?

Cool, huh?

Practicing Your Penmanship

1. Why do you think it is important to read the Bible in large chunks instead of just picking and choosing small sections? What kind of problems can you see the "pick-and-choose" method causing?
2. Looking at the story of David and Goliath, does the fact that in God's big story David will be the ancestor of Jesus impact the way you view the story? How?
3. We listed a number of questions to ask of a passage:
    *   Why is this here?
    *   What is the genre?
    *   What was the original author's focus and intention?
    *   What did the original audience hear?

    Which one do you find most interesting? How do you think it could impact your reading?
4. There is a big difference between believing a Bible passage can say different things to different people, and believing a Bible passage can have different applications for different people. Why is this distinction important?

17 PRAYER

At one time I really thought my life direction was to be a professor. During that time I took a course at a rather prestigious seminary. The class was on the Septuagint, which is the Greek translation of the Hebrew Bible. The class was interesting, but the professor was fascinating.

He was born in Africa, drove a motorcycle, was extremely blunt and forceful, and knew the Bible in the original languages about as well as anyone I've ever met. He also occasionally dabbled in pastoral ministry.

Did I mention yet that He was agnostic?

Yep. He said he "bracketed the supernatural," choosing not to even attempt to answer the question of whether God existed. He knew the Bible extremely well, but only at the "What it says" level, maybe occasionally dipping into the "What it means" zone. But he could never get to the "What it means to me" level, because the Holy Spirit wasn't guiding him into truth.[136]

It is important to remember that reading the Bible the way we discussed is not a purely (or even primarily) intellectual exercise. It is spiritual.

That's where prayer comes in.

Now, when I say "prayer" I know I scare a lot of people. Some of us grew up with Brother So-and-So, Master of the Impressive Prayer.[137] Lots of thee's and thou's and big words, proclaimed in a tone somewhere between inspiring and terrifying. Sort of a mashup of Darth Vader reading *The Complete Works of Shakespeare*.

---

[136] John 16:13
[137] Also should have been in *The Princess Bride*

91

Others of us have been intimidated by one of God's BFF's, a person who makes it seem like Jesus sits down with them over coffee and always shares exact details of what He wants them to do in every situation. "I was going to buy Corn Flakes, but Jesus told me I needed to buy Cheerios today."

Then when we pray for ourselves, instead of getting clear instructions over brunch, it seems more like trying to read fine print reflected in a dark, cloudy mirror.[138] Or when we're asked to pray in a group, our voice sounds more like C3PO than James Earl Jones. And we're convinced we must be doing prayer wrong.

Then there's the problem of how and when and where. On my knees at four in the morning or standing with arms outstretched on a beach at sunset?

Well, first, I don't think prayer is supposed to be scary, or intimidating, and definitely not procedural or impressive. When Jesus taught His followers to pray, He said to start with "Our father...." And while not all fathers live into the ideal, the father's job is to make us feel loved not afraid.

So, how and why do we pray? From my personal experience, I've found four primary types of prayer are important in my life. We'll start with the obvious one.

Asking

How about we make this first type of prayer as un-scary as possible? Write down a list of everything that you're even a little bit worried about, as well as the things you're most thankful for. Now, once a day, find a time and place to talk to God about your list. When something comes off the list, be sure to move it from the concern section to the thankful section, at least for a while.

Sound too simple? Paul didn't think so. He put it this way:

Don't worry about anything; instead, pray about everything.

---

138 1 Corinthians 13:12

Tell God what you need, and thank him for all he has done.[139]

Your list will grow and develop with time. God will make you aware of things that you'll want to add to your list, like maybe human trafficking, or problems in your community, or areas of your life where you want to see Him work. You may add so many things you need to have different lists for different days, or discover an app that helps you organize your list and also make you aware of other needs.[140]

By the way, it's okay that you'll be doing most of the talking. The key is to understand that God is present and that He will make you aware of the things He wants you to know.[141]

Now, what physical position should you have while discussing your list? I've found two primary considerations: life situation and personal attitude.

There have been times in my life where I've had extremely long commutes to work. During those times, I've experienced some great prayer times while driving. I was less stressed than I would have been trying to get it done before I got to my car. I've also had periods where I needed to focus more on God's transcendence, His holiness and otherness. During those times, I've prayed on my knees. But the majority of my prayer times have been sitting in a chair. The important thing isn't my physical position but my attitude. Many times I've changed my physical position or the way I handle my list just because my time with God was starting to feel stale, and I figured a change might spice things up a bit.

And the right voice to use while praying? Yours, of course.

If you want more help, there are tons of books on prayer. The key is not to let any of them intimidate you. The "how" of asking prayer is much less important than developing the habit. Get your list together, pick a time and place, and get started.

---

139 Philippians 4:6 (NLT)

140 I use one called Prayermate.

141 No promise about Cheerios or Corn Flakes.

Aligning Prayer

Have you ever loved a movie right up to the end, then hated the ending so much it ruined the whole thing? Or have you ever enjoyed a TV series, but the final episode left you totally dissatisfied?

We're all like that. We put a ton of value on the endings, even to the point we often disregard the value of the journey that got us to that ending.

That's a problem. Even though Christians talk a lot about Heaven, the Christian life isn't as much about the ending as it is the journey. It's about being the person God wants me to be right now, at this stage of my development and growth, and doing the things He wants me to do today. The goal isn't some spectacular ending. The goal is to continuously be where God wants me to be each day.

That's where Alignment prayer comes in. It starts when our daily prayer and Bible reading grows from being about learning cool things about God and talking to God about our list, to learning things God wants us to apply to our lives and praying about how God wants us to align our lives with Him each day.

Eventually, there will be times when that alignment takes on more urgent tones. Like when we have an important decision to make, or God seems to be making us discontent with some area of our life. Then the Alignment prayer moves from our personal worship time to, well, all the time. We find ourselves almost constantly asking God to make His will clear to us.

This would probably be a good time to de-mystify prayer a little bit. When it comes to serious alignment prayers, people can get a little squirrelly. They start asking for God to write something in the sky, or speak directly from heaven, preferably in a really deep voice. That's not the normal way He helps us align with His will. Sure, sometimes He speaks in a still, small voice into our hearts, and we just know it was

Him speaking. But frequently, He uses another technique. As we pray and ponder and talk with others about the decision, God does something almost unbelievable. He lets us figure it out for ourselves.

Seriously.

Here's what James says about it.

If any of you lacks wisdom, you should ask God, who gives generously to all without finding fault, and it will be given to you.[142]

Trust Him, be open to whatever He wants you to do, then do what makes the most sense. Really. That's how it works most of the time. No angels at the foot of the bed. No dissecting of sheep livers. Believe Him enough to trust that what seems right is right. (Which takes a lot more faith than taking the word of an angel standing at the foot of your bed.) Sometimes I'll ask people what they would advise a person in their situation, then suggest they take their own advice.

If He wants you to do something that isn't the logical choice, He'll tell you. Once Peter saw Jesus walking on water and wanted to join Him. He called to Jesus, *"Lord, if it's really you, tell me to come to you, walking on the water."*[143] In other words Peter is saying, "Jesus, wisdom says stay in the boat, but if you want me out there, tell me and I'll do it." So Peter walked on water. And if God wants us to do something that out of the boat, er, box, He'll tell us. And if He doesn't, then do what wisdom says.

When I moved to North Carolina to start our church, there was no writing in the sky, no voices from heaven, or even a still, small voice. There was a pastor of a failing new church (me) with no other viable options to feed my family and stay in ministry, except for an offer from a friend to plant a church where one was needed. Other people felt God telling them I was the person for the job, but since God knew

---

[142] James 1:5 (NIV)
[143] Matthew 14:28 (NLT)

that wisdom would get me where He wanted me, He didn't have to use any mystical methods. We packed up and moved, and God's been doing amazing things ever since.

Remember, God wants you to know His will even more than you want to know it. So trust that as long as you are sincerely seeking it, He will reveal it. However He chooses.

Continual Connection Prayer

One advantage of Alignment Prayer is it moves our prayer lives out of just a once-a-day thing and into our twenty-four-hour-a-day lives, and moves us toward this next type, Continual Connection Prayer.

One of the shortest verses in the Bible is also one of the most challenging. *"Pray continually."*[144] If you try to take your Asking prayer list around with you all day, constantly reminding God of what you're concerned about, you're going to fail. Even our Aligning prayers fail the constancy test when we're not facing a critical decision.

So what is this verse asking of us? It's something a guy called Brother Lawrence called, "practicing the presence of God." It's moving throughout your day, constantly aware of His presence. Sometimes talking, sometimes silent, but always aware. As Dallas Willard put it, "Spiritual people are not those who engage in spiritual practices; they are those who draw their life from a conversational relationship with God."[145]

This is a challenging area of prayer. I personally struggle with it. But I've found that whenever I'm even a little successful, the rewards are enormous. The Book of Psalms says, *"In your presence there is fullness of joy,"*[146] and *"Surely you have granted him unending blessings and made him glad with the joy of your presence."*[147] My personal experience affirms this, and makes

---

[144] 1 Thessalonians 5:17 (NIV)
[145] Dallas Willard, *Hearing God*
[146] Psalm 16:11 (ESV)
[147] Psalm 21:6 (NIV)

Continual Connection Prayer well worth pursuing.

Wrestling Prayer

We have four dogs. (Yes, four.) Winter is our American Eskimo, a medium-sized alpha-male fur ball. Genevieve is a mutt, but a small one. She's about the size of a loaf of bread, but don't tell her that. She's liable to lead a coup to overthrow Winter any day now. Hershey is my wife's Shih Tzu. Spoiled rotten, dumb as a box of rocks,[148] and even smaller than Genevieve. The pound said Misty, our fourth dog, would be a small dog. They were wrong. Really, really wrong. She weighs over 80 pounds, most of it fat.

While Winter stays above the fray, the other three like to wrestle. Especially when there is something we want to watch on TV. The fighting started when the little ones were puppies. The three would wrestle for hours.

But here's the thing. Misty never really wins and the little ones never, ever get hurt. Which made me think. Maybe what they're doing isn't just wrestling. What if Misty, the older female, is really training the little ones with what looks like fighting?

I'm pretty sure that's what is happening. She is teaching them skills and making them stronger, not trying to defeat them.

I believe sometimes God does that with us. He places a problem in front of us that is bigger than our faith, then He lets us wrestle with it and with Him. As the contest continues, we end up growing stronger as He increases our faith to match the challenge.

I call this Wrestling Prayer after Jacob who literally wrestled with God. A clear sign we are engaged in this kind of praying is that the answer does not come quickly or easily. When I've been in wrestling prayer situations, I've often prayed what Jacob prayed. "*I will not let you go unless you bless*

---

148 My wife disputes this analysis.

me.[149]

This is the most difficult of the four types of prayer. It's one you don't initiate, and it's one you won't enjoy.

It is also the rarest. And it is the one where I have experienced the most intense periods of spiritual growth in my life.

Defining a Win

One final thought on prayer and Bible reading. How often should you do it?

Of course, the simple answer is "daily."

The problem is, we all set out to spend time with God every day, but life rarely cooperates. Kids get sick, or we get sick, or we oversleep, or we come home too tired or, well, we just get busy. If our goal is to have personal worship (another way of saying prayer and Bible reading) every day, we'll get discouraged because we will keep missing days.

I heard another pastor give an excellent suggestion on how to keep from getting discouraged. Define your win. Before you even start spending time with God, figure out how many times a week you'll classify as a success. Then count each individual week as either a win or a loss. When I win a week, hooray. When I don't, well, I'll get it next week.

How many days a week should I define as a win? Personally, I use five. Believe it or not, Sunday is a really hard day for me to spend the kind of quality time with God that I want. Even when I get that one, life is going to interfere one or two days a week. So I define a win as five daily times of personal worship a week, and recommend that for others (though, of course, you're free to define your own).

Five days a week (or whatever you choose to define as a win) means you're learning about God and letting Him speak to you from the Bible on a regular basis. It means you're discussing your list of concerns with Him often enough to

---

[149] Genesis 32:26 (NIV)

feel like it's making a difference, and you're keeping yourself aligned with Him.

And if you can "win" most of the weeks of the year, you are allowing God's Spirit to work with you to develop a faith that isn't built exclusively on what others tell you, but a faith that you develop in partnership with Him. Together, you will be writing your faith in your own handwriting, developing a faith worthy of your entire life.

Practicing Your Penmanship

1. Have you ever felt guilty about prayer? How much of that guilt was legitimate, and how much was based on improper assumptions about prayer?

2. Does the idea of Asking prayer seem too simple to you? Why?

3. Have you ever had a time of Aligning Prayer or Wrestling Prayer? What was that like? If not, what do you think it would be like? Does the idea of either one scare you?

4. What could you do to facilitate Continual Connection Prayer in your life?

18 THE SECRET SAUCE

Jesus said a lot of difficult things. Some were simply hard to figure out. I've been reading the Bible for years, and I still scratch my head about some of His statements.

But the really difficult sayings are the ones I have no trouble understanding, but struggle to implement.

Whoever does not bear his own cross and come after me cannot be my disciple.[150]

No one who puts a hand to the plow and looks back is fit for service in the kingdom of God.[151]

So you also, when you have done all that you were commanded, say, 'We are unworthy servants; we have only done what was our duty.[152]

The level of commitment Jesus called for was staggering. And life changing.

But seek first his kingdom and his righteousness, and all these things will be given to you as well.[153]

When I really recognized the truth and power of that statement, it took my level of commitment to a new level and transformed my life. Everyone who knew me noticed the difference.

Problem is, a lot of the time we don't want to talk about commitment. We're afraid it will scare people off. (You'll notice I saved it until the end of the book.)

---

150 Luke 14:27 (ESV)
151 Luke 9:62 (NIV)
152 Luke 17:10 (ESV)
153 Matthew 6:33a (NIV)

While commitment may not be the first thing to mention when talking to someone about the faith, I believe it is the top-secret, life-changing super ingredient of faith. How far you'll go in your faith, how much impact you'll have in bringing God's principles into the world, and even how much you'll enjoy your faith are all tied to how committed you are. Low commitment, low impact, low joy. High commitment, high impact, high joy.

It's as simple as that.

But what does commitment look like in a Christian? Is it about dressing a certain way all the time? Speaking in religious jargon? Saying "bless you" to people who haven't even sneezed?

I don't think so (though your commitment may well impact what you wear and how you speak). I believe commitment manifests itself in five key areas: how you think, how you spend your time, how you use your abilities, how you manage your resources, and one more commitment I'll tell you about at the end.

Resource Management

Honesty time. Another word for resource management is giving. And since no one wants to talk about money, let's start there and get it over with.

Commitment in resource management is about putting your money (and everything else you own) where your mouth is. If I say I'm a Christian and my life is all about advancing God's Kingdom, how I handle my resources should reflect that commitment.

But the thing, with money, just like all these commitments, the bottom line is trust. How we handle our money is both a window into how much we trust God and a tool to help us grow in our trust.

If I truly believe that God is the ultimate source for all I have, then giving Him a percentage of what I earn shouldn't be that big a deal. And if reading that statement makes me squirm uncontrollably, it could well be a sign that my level of trust in God might need some pumping up.

Thankfully God gave us a tool to grow our trust. The Prophet Malachi explained it this way:

> *Bring the whole tithe into the storehouse, that there may be food in my house. Test me in this,"* says the LORD *Almighty,* *"and see if I will not throw open the floodgates of heaven and pour out so much blessing that there will not be room enough to store it.*[154]

Basically, God is saying, if you don't trust me, test me. Start tithing (that means giving ten percent of your income) and see if I don't over-bless you for it. He doesn't say He'll match your money with His money (or double your money, or anything like that). He says that if you're willing to trust Him with your money, which you really don't need, He'll provide what you really do need. Food, clothing, and the things money can buy, as well as love, joy, peace and other things it cannot.

Now, the thought of giving ten percent of your income may be staggering. That's okay. If ten percent is overwhelming (and it is for a lot of people), start with one or two. See if as you trust Him in your giving, He doesn't flood you with good.

As you learn this, you will start to see that the rest of your possessions—and the way you make all your financial decisions—should be driven by trusting God and advancing His Kingdom principles.

Have a car? Maybe God wants to use it for more than taking kids to dance class. Maybe you could take youth bowling or a widow to a doctor's appointment.

Have a house? Maybe it could become the safe place where the kids in the neighborhood can play, or the host site for a small group.

---

[154] Malachi 3:10 (NIV)

"What do you have that God hasn't given you?"[155] If He gave it to you, He wants you to enjoy it,[156] but He also wants you to use it.

Now here's the coolest part about this giving test. A lot of times we believe that to change our actions, we first need to change our attitudes. Instead of giving, we say we'll pray about it. Instead of using our resources for God, we ask God to give us an attitude that desires to give.

Jesus, who understands people a lot better than we do, saw it differently. He said, *"For where your treasure is, there your heart will be also."*[157]

Two important things to note about that saying. First, it's not a command, it's an observation of truth. He's not saying to put your heart where your treasure is. He's saying your heart follows your treasure. Say there's this corporation you've never heard of and don't care about in the least. Then one day you read a blog about the company and decide to buy some of their stock.

Now, you care about that company. You read every article about it, and sweat its every stock market up and down. Until you sell the stock. Then your heart moves to a new company. Your heart follows your treasure.

The second, more subtle thing about Jesus' statement about your heart following your treasure is that it gives us a formula for changing our hearts. Put your money and resources where you want your heart to be, and your heart will follow.

Want to be more concerned about exploited children? Start giving to a ministry that rescues kids (and give enough to command a chunk of your heart). Want to care more about the hungry people in your community? Give an evening a month to a local food bank. (As we'll discuss in a bit, time is just another form of treasure.) Want to care more about

---

[155] 1 Corinthians 4:7 (NLT)

[156] He does love us after all.

[157] Matthew 6:21 (ESV)

God's Kingdom in your community? Start giving to your local church.

Those acts of moving your treasure will give you a great head start on the second area of commitment.

Committed Thinking

Hard truth time. Your brain is broken.

It's okay. Mine is, too.

When we say that we're fallen creatures, that fallenness is centered in our brains. If we truly want to be the people God wants us to be, the necessary transformation must occur in our minds.

> *Do not conform to the pattern of this world, but be transformed by the renewing of your mind. Then you will be able to test and approve what God's will is—his good, pleasing and perfect will.*[158]

That's why following a list of rules won't lead to a satisfying Christian life or give you a faith that is in your own handwriting. Following rules without letting God transform your mind leads either to frustration, legalism, judgmentalism, or all of the above.

We need to think differently.

Which isn't easy. It takes almost constant commitment.

The Ten Commandments say not to commit adultery. Jesus took it up a notch and said to look at a woman with desire is the same as adultery,[159] so men must train themselves to think differently about women.

The Ten Commandments say not to covet other people's stuff,[160] so we have to train ourselves to think differently about other people and their possessions. Paul then took it up a notch, telling people who are prone to stealing to quit

---

[158] Romans 12:2 (NIV)

[159] Matthew 5:28

[160] Exodus 20:17

stealing, get a job, and start giving stuff away.[161]

Behind both of those, and most other issues like this, is to intentionally change the way we think about everything. We intentionally change the way we view people. *We have stopped evaluating others from a human point of view.*[162] We intentionally change the way we view situations. And as we have already seen, we intentionally change the way we view possessions.

This change can be summed up in one phrase. We commit to viewing everything from an eternal perspective. Other people aren't there to be used, they are individuals made in the image of God and created for a relationship with Him. My responsibility, with every person I encounter, is to try to help them toward that purpose.[163]

The situations in which I find myself aren't accidental or even coincidental. They are providential opportunities for God to transform me, to use me to accomplish His mission, or both.

Possessions are not measurements of my worth, they are tools God allows me to use to accomplish His purposes.

Now, my fallen brain fights me on this one. Daily. Selfishness attacks my view of others. Circumstances drive my emotions. Stuff becomes a way for me to feel better about myself.

How do I win? Not by simply overpowering my natural inclinations. They are too strong. I win by changing my actions (as we saw with possessions) and allowing God to change me through my new actions.

This will become clearer as we look at the third commitment, the commitment of time.

Time Commitment

If you think about it, time and money have a lot in common. We value both highly. Both can be spent well or

---

[161] Ephesians 4:28
[162] 2 Corinthians 5:16 (NLT)
[163] 2 Corinthians 5:20

wasted. And God's technique for training us is very similar in both.

When God wants to teach us to trust Him with our money, He asks us to give a percentage of our income (10% is the suggestion) to advance His work. When He wants to teach us to trust Him with our time, He gives us instructions on how to handle a certain percentage, in this case fourteen.

Seriously. God instructs us to take off one day a week. It's called the Sabbath, and God considers it so important it made His Top Ten list. (Tithing didn't make the list.)

Think about that for a second. There are over 600 instructions in the Old Testament. God narrowed them down to ten, and wrote them on stone tablets for Moses to give to the Israelites. Most of them are obvious. No gods before Him. Honor your parents. Don't lie, or steal, or murder, or even covet.

And stuck in the middle is one unlike the rest: Take one day off a week. This is the one commandment that isn't focused on God (like the first few commandments) or other people (like the second half). This one is focused on us. Jesus even said that this particular commandment was in there for our benefit.[164]

The Ten Commandments are actually in the Bible twice,[165] and interestingly, the explanation given for the Sabbath is different both times. In each list it starts out by saying to remember the Sabbath, then gives some details into what that means. Don't do any work. Don't let the people in your household work. Don't even let your animals work. Then each gives a reason for the Sabbath. And the reasons are different.

In Exodus it says:

"For in six days the LORD made the heavens and the earth, the sea, and all that is in them, but he rested on the seventh day. Therefore the LORD blessed the Sabbath day and made

---

[164] Mark 2:27

[165] Exodus 20 and Deuteronomy 5

it holy."[166]

Then Deuteronomy gives this explanation:

"Remember that you were slaves in Egypt and that the LORD your God brought you out of there with a mighty hand and an outstretched arm. Therefore the LORD your God has commanded you to observe the Sabbath day."[167]

Exodus reminds us that we can honor God by taking a day off because He created and controls the universe. Deuteronomy says we can take the day off because God is protecting and guiding us toward His plan for our lives (and that plan does not include slavery to our desires or our past). We can trust God enough to rest one day a week because the job of CEO of the Universe is taken, and is in very capable hands (not ours). And our lives won't spin out of control because those same hands are guiding both the stars and our future.

Which teaches us a valuable lesson. In the same way giving God a percent of our income teaches us we can trust Him with all our possessions, the Sabbath teaches us that if we can trust God for one day a week, we can trust him for all seven. We can schedule our entire lives with Him in mind.

That means we can say Yes to things that advance His Kingdom, and No to things that wear us down or distract us from what He is trying to accomplish in our lives and in His world.

Which brings us to the fourth commitment area, and my cool technique to make a person taller.

Committing Our Abilities

I call it "what gets your butt off the seat."

You can be having a conversation with a person who seems completely disinterested. In everything.

---

[166] Exodus 20:11 (NIV)
[167] Deuteronomy 5:15 (NIV)

Then you bring up a topic. Children. Or comic books. Or animals. Or feeding the hungry.

Suddenly, the person's eyes light up. The conversation gets animated. And they literally seem to grow taller as their butts come slightly off their chair. They lean toward you, and the person who didn't want to talk now shows no sign of ever shutting up.

We all have them. The things that really matter to us. For me it's helping churches reach people and advance God's Kingdom. It's teaching the Bible. It's West Virginia University football and basketball.

Here's the cool part. For the most part, God inspires those passions. He wants us to have things we're excited about, and even moves to develop them.

Why? Because those are the areas where He wants us to work to advance His Kingdom. When it comes to looking for your purpose in life, that excitement is like the big X on a treasure map. Dig here.

You may be saying, "Sure I get that God wants you to be excited about teaching the Bible, but do you really think He cares about your football team?"

In a word, yes. First, because West Virginia is "Almost Heaven," and more importantly because it is a doorway, a connection. There are people who I can get to know because we share that passion. Some of them God may need me to help through a tough time, or to tell them about a relationship with Jesus.

It's crucial to understand that writing your faith in your own handwriting isn't exclusively—or even primarily—about you. It's also about the lives God wants you to impact, the causes He wants you to advance, and the principles He wants you to take a stand for. Here's how Paul puts it in 2 Corinthians:

> *Christ's love compels us, because we are convinced that one died for all, and therefore all died. And he died for all, that those who live should no longer live for themselves but for him who*

died for them and was raised again.

So from now on we regard no one from a worldly point of view. Though we once regarded Christ in this way, we do so no longer. Therefore, if anyone is in Christ, the new creation has come: The old has gone, the new is here! All this is from God, who reconciled us to himself through Christ and gave us the ministry of reconciliation: that God was reconciling the world to himself in Christ, not counting people's sins against them. And he has committed to us the message of reconciliation. We are therefore Christ's ambassadors, as though God were making his appeal through us. We implore you on Christ's behalf: Be reconciled to God.[168]

Powerful stuff.

As we grow to be more like Jesus, we're supposed to live more and more for Him and for others instead of for ourselves. Now that doesn't sound like fun, but here's the rub. It's what we were made for. For that reason, we get more joy from living for God's purposes than we do from living selfishly. As Jesus put it, *"If you cling to your life, you will lose it; but if you give up your life for me, you will find it."*[169]

That means we're supposed to stop viewing people through the lens of "what can they do for me?" and switch to an eternal perspective that asks, "How can I best help them move into the life God has for them?" Or, again, as Jesus put it, *"Do to others what you would have them do to you."*[170]

How does it work? It sounds simple, but plenty of people have tried and failed to find what God wants them to do. I think that's because we begin by asking the wrong question and by looking in the wrong place. We act like God is hiding His will from us and challenging us to find it, when in fact it's one of the things He most wants to show us.

So people stress out and look all over the world for their

---

[168] 2 Corinthians 5:14-20 (NIV)

[169] Matthew 10:39 (NLT)

[170] Matthew 7:12 (NIV)

purpose, never thinking to look closer to home. Instead, start with who you are and where you are.

Look in your local community and look in your faith community. (That's another way of saying, "your church.") What can you do to help? Don't wait for a lightning bolt from God, look for an opportunity.

At our church, we call this serving out of need. You may or may not have a great passion to help people find a parking spot, but someone has to direct them. Someone has to help them register their kids for the children's ministry. It needs done, you can do it, so do it. Introverts fill different needs in the church than extroverts. Tech geeks fill different needs than Luddites.[171]

The second place to look is inside yourself. What are your interests? What are you good at? What are your passions? What injustices make you most angry? What problems do you most want to solve? What makes your butt come off the seat?

Sometimes, as you're serving because there is a need you develop a passion. Sometimes an article or book awakens a passion. And sometimes there are things you've just always been passionate about. Chances are very good that God is guiding that passion.[172] Instead of asking God to give you a passion to do something for Him, ask Him to show you how you can use the skills and passions you already have.

And expect Him to answer.

But be careful. There is a fifth commitment that can maximize the impact of all the others.

The Commitment to Say Yes.

This fifth commitment could make you very uncomfortable. I call it the Automatic Yes.

The Automatic Yes is agreeing that your answer will be Yes before God even asks the question. When God shows

---

[171] A Luddite is someone who hates technology—but for our discussion is still seeking God.

[172] Assuming it fits in with God's standards and principles

me something from the Bible that I know I need to apply to my life, the answer is, "Yes, I will do my best to apply it." If God makes me aware in a way I know is coming from Him that I need to do something, go somewhere, or even quit something, the answer is "Yes."

I'm not going to pray about it. I'm not going to seek counsel, unless it's how best to obey. If I'm sure God is telling me to do something, the answer is pre-determined. Yes.

The Automatic Yes takes all of these commitments we've discussed to the next level. Instead of our obedience being a piecemeal affair, where we do the things we're comfortable with and skip the uncomfortable ones, God knows we're all in, that He can count on us.

Does He want us to utilize a resource He gave us in a way that will challenge our faith? Yes.

Do I need to change my attitude toward a group of people, or toward a certain issue? Change is on its way.

Do I need to rearrange my schedule to better reflect His priorities? Let's cancel some appointments.

Is God awakening a passion in me that will require some major life adjustments? The answer is yes.

And because of that, God can do things through us and take us to places beyond anything we've ever dreamed.[173]

Practicing Your Penmanship

1. On a scale of 1 to 10, how would you rate your overall commitment to following Jesus? Do you believe you need to increase that rating?

2. Of the five commitments, Resource Management, Committed Thinking, Time Commitment, Ability Commitment, and the Automatic Yes, which is your strongest? Which needs the most work?

3. Name one specific thing you can do to increase your commitment in each of the five areas.

---

[173] Ephesians 3:20

19 TEMPTATIONS AND TRIALS

So, we have the five commitments. I think you can see how valuable they can be. But before we tie everything together and put a bow on the entire book, I need to tell you one more reason commitment is so important.

As you're growing into the person God created you to be, there are two types of challenges you're going to face. Both are very difficult, and if you're not committed, either one can stall or even stop you from writing your faith in your own handwriting.

Here's the kicker. They are complete opposites in their sources, their purposes, and our responses. Matter of fact, one is your primary obstacle to spiritual growth, while the other is God's primary tool to help your develop your faith.

These two things are trials and temptations.

A lot of people use those two words interchangeably, but they shouldn't. They represent two totally different concepts. The Bible's Book of James sums the whole situation up pretty clearly.

First, he addresses trials:

> *Consider it pure joy, my brothers and sisters, whenever you face trials of many kinds, because you know that the testing of your faith produces perseverance. Let perseverance finish its work so that you may be mature and complete, not lacking anything.*[174]

Trials are difficult circumstances that God allows into our lives for the purpose of helping us grow to spiritual maturity. Our job in trials is to endure, even though our desire is to escape.

---

[174] James 1:2-4 (NIV)

A few verses later, he addresses the temptations:

When tempted, no one should say, "God is tempting me." For God cannot be tempted by evil, nor does he tempt anyone; but each person is tempted when they are dragged away by their own evil desire and enticed. Then, after desire has conceived, it gives birth to sin; and sin, when it is full-grown, gives birth to death.[175]

Temptations come from our own sinful nature, often with an assist from the enemy. The purpose of a temptation is to destroy us, and though our desire is to embrace the temptation, what we need to do is to run away.[176]

See, exact opposites. Escape temptations, endure trials. If we yield to temptations, we'll be damaged or destroyed. If we endure trials we'll grow.

So how do we tell them apart? How do we identify which we're going through so we can respond appropriately?

It's not that complicated. Do the opposite of what you want to do.

Really. Our desire when we're undergoing trials, when things are going badly, is to get away. We want to do whatever it takes to make the trial end. We want it all to be over with as soon as possible. We want to run. So stay. That's a trial. You need to endure it.

Let's say your finances have gotten tight. Very tight. What do you daydream about? Anything that will make the problem go away. Winning the lottery. Getting a big promotion. Running away and hoping no one finds you. Anything that will let you escape the tension caused by the trial.

What should you do? Ride it out. Learn to trust God in the trial. Give Him a chance to work before you bail yourself out with a credit card.

Temptation, as we've said, is the opposite. When tempted,

---

[175] James 1:13-15 (NIV)
[176] Amos 5:14; 1 Corinthians 6:18; 2 Timothy 2:22

our desire is to move closer to the temptation. Say you have an attractive co-worker, someone who is totally not your spouse. You want to hang around with the person, just be near them. Not doing anything wrong, just standing close to the temptation. That's our desire. What should we do? Run away. Put as much distance between you and it as you can manage.

Now, frequently temptations tag along in trials. We're tempted to do something wrong to get out of the trial. Like when the pressures of the financial trial mounts, and we may be tempted to compromise our integrity—lie on an expense form, cheat on our taxes—to make the trial less severe.

But, when you're in a trial, and the temptations come, remember the Sabbath.

Seriously. The Sabbath teaches us that God is in control of the universe and our lives. Which means, if bad things are happening, God probably isn't causing them, but He is allowing them. And He is allowing the problems for our good. He wants us to become the people He made us to be, and He knows the trial will advance that process. Or, as I like to say, "If it got to you, God let it through." So don't cheat the process by giving in to a temptation. Endure the trial. God is working all of it *for the good of those who love him, who have been called according to his purpose.*[177]

Practicing Your Penmanship

1. Try to state the difference between trials and temptations in your own words.
2. What is one of the biggest trials you've ever been through? What lessons did you learn from it?
3. One other big difference between trials and temptations is that while trials change drastically over time, temptations often recur in our lives. We tend to have weak areas, and temptations regularly target those same weaknesses. What is one of your recurring temptations? Have you found any specific strategies to deal with it?

[177] Romans 8:28 (NIV)

20 IN YOUR OWN HANDWRITING

When I was twelve, my dad took me to a Southern Gospel concert.[178] When one of the singers asked those of us who wanted to have a relationship with Jesus to come to the front of the gym, I went.

When I was in college, my dad was serving as a pastor and going through some rough times because of his commitment to advancing God's Kingdom. I asked myself if I believed as strongly as he did, and had to admit the answer was no. I decided to do something about it and ended up transferring from a major college studying electrical engineering to a private Christian school to study... honestly, I had no idea. I just knew God wanted me to go, so I went.

The following summer, during a church service, God's Spirit spoke very clearly into my mind and heart that He wanted me to become a pastor. I'd never had an experience like it before, and haven't had one since, but after some wrestling about what exactly that would look like in my life, I said yes.

Throughout my life, God has shaped me, guided me, and led me to do things differently than the way people around me were doing them. It's often been difficult, and many times it would have been easier to let my faith be written in other people's handwriting.

But God made me stubborn. While holding to the core teachings of the faith, I've read the Bible for myself, listened to teachers to hear what God wants to say to me, prayed for Him to guide me, and tried to stay committed with my

---

[178] Not my favorite style of music then or now, but God works in mysterious ways.

resources, my attitudes, my time, and my abilities.

And I'm not done yet. I hope to continue writing my faith in my own handwriting, listening to whatever God wants to say to me, and always trying to answer Yes.

My path may not have been the easiest, and it may not look like anyone else's. That's fine. I believe that's the way it's supposed to be.

But now it's your turn.

Your faith is waiting to be written.

I have come that they may have life,
and have it to the full.

John 10:10 (NIV)

Appendices

CHOOSING A CHURCH

Among the most important decisions you'll make is which church you'll connect with. If you're still making your initial faith decision, the wrong church can push you to a wrong decision. If you're a new believer or seeking to re-write your childhood faith in your own handwriting, the church you choose will be a major force in shaping (or re-shaping) your faith. And even for more experienced Christians, a church can stunt your growth or help you move to a greater faith than you'd dreamed possible.

And remember, this decision is personal. God has made you unique, and your church choice should enhance that uniqueness, not conform you to some human pattern. Your focus should be on pleasing God and finding His will for you.

In my immediate family, one of my sisters is comfortable in the same style church she grew up in, while the other worships and serves in a totally different environment. The church I pastor is radically different from both, and I think my baby brother is still working out his fit. Your job is to find your own God-designed path, not focus on the approval of anyone else.

When it comes to your church decision, I think there are five things to consider: worship focus, worship style, church calling, church doctrine, and your connection.

We discussed **worship focus** earlier in the book. You may remember the concepts of God's Immanence (God is near.) and His Transcendence (God is other.). As we mentioned, these strongly influence worship. Do you most easily worship in surroundings that point to God's majesty or His proximity? Do incense and stained glass draw you to worship, or do less formal settings make you feel closer to God?

Worship style is different from focus. Do you worship best with upbeat, contemporary music or with pipe organs and traditional hymns? Acoustic or electric guitars? Dresses and suits, or jeans and t-shirts? I believe people can worship God in all these diverse styles, but that doesn't mean you personally can. Some styles will help you worship, some won't. Some could even discourage you from worship. While I think this is probably the least important of the five considerations, it is real.

The one consideration that I think most people don't even recognize is **church calling**, but I think it might be the most important.

In his book *Blind Spots: Becoming a Courageous, Compassionate, and Commissioned Church*, Collin Hansen defines three types of churches based on their calling. Courageous churches take stands. Whether it's a cultural issue or a doctrinal dispute, courageous churches relish speaking truth into a situation.

Compassionate churches seek out the downtrodden. They feed the poor, love the unlovable, and try their best to be the healing hands of Jesus toward anyone who is hurting.

Commissioned churches focus on the Great Commission. They are all about helping unbelievers find their way to Jesus, and are always on the lookout for the best methods of communicating the Good News.

Obviously, Jesus calls every church to do all three, but churches tend to migrate toward their strength. While I doubt any church member would say their church ignores one of these, it doesn't take long to tell which of these three each church considers its calling. Our church has a real heart for compassion, and does its best to stand for truth, but if you cut us we bleed the Great Commission.

Here's the thing. As you develop your faith, you will probably find yourself drawn more toward one of these callings than the other. For you to fully live into what God wants to do in your life, your church has to support your calling. Our church makes a concerted effort to wed Commission and Compassion. We think advancing the Gospel includes transforming cultures to better reflect God's values. We have plenty of members who have a primary calling toward compassion and they fit in well with our church's mission and vision.

The same can't be said about people who are called to the Courageous church. Our almost-overwhelming passion to reach people and advance God's Kingdom means we don't take public stands on as many issues as the purely courageous like. People with this calling tend to leave our church eventually. Hopefully, they can find a Courageous church where they can more fully write their faith.

One key thing to remember about calling is that the only wrong answer is the one that doesn't match you. The world needs Courageous, Compassionate, and Commissioned churches. And all three need each other. Without the Courageous churches watching our doctrinal backsides, the Compassionate and Commissioned churches can wander into serious error. Without the prodding of the Compassionate churches, the other two can become cold and uncaring. And without the passionate pushing of the Commissioned churches, the other churches can become inwardly focused.

The key isn't which one is right. The key is which one (or which combination) is right for you.

A fourth consideration, and one that is directly tied to how far along you are in your spiritual development process is **church doctrine**. If you're just getting started, you probably don't have strongly developed beliefs on any of the secondary doctrinal issues. While you hopefully understand the importance of the Deity of Christ, you may have no opinion whatsoever on, for instance, the "proper" method of baptism. Rest assured, the church you connect with will have an opinion. Before you connect, make sure you have at least some peace about the church's doctrinal stands. If you feel misgivings here, that could be God nudging you in a different direction.

If you have been a Christian for a while, you may well have strong opinions on certain theological issues. Make sure your views are compatible (not necessarily identical, but compatible) with the church you're considering. You can write this down. You're not going to change their mind, and they're going to try to change yours, intentionally or not. Joining a church with the idea of changing them is just as bad an idea as getting married with a plan to change your prospective spouse.

The final consideration is **Your Connection**. Can you see yourself belonging here? While the church's job isn't to make you comfortable, a certain level of comfort with the people of a church and its culture is vital. If you are considering a church but can't see yourself working in and with the people of that church, if you don't see yourself confidently giving your money or your time, or if you can't imagine inviting people to that church, keep looking.

Of course, there is one more thing to consider. Churches come in lots of flavors. Perfect is not one of them. Churches are composed of screwed up people (like you), so they are all imperfect. Usually massively so (again, like you). Perfection and connection are not the same thing.

What if you can't find a good church fit in your area? Pick the one that comes closest and try to make it work. You need other believers to truly thrive, even if the match is far from perfect, and quite often that imperfect fit works out better than you'd expect.

You can also look online for a church that broadcasts its services. An online church service might make up for what's lacking in a local church. And if you just can't connect, pray that God sends someone to your area to start a brand new church where you can serve and grow.

WHICH BIBLE SHOULD I READ?

Not that long ago, this was a much more stress-filled decision. Choosing a Bible meant going to a Christian bookstore, spending a fair amount of money, and then sticking with a single Bible for years and years. Some people used one Bible for their entire lives, and a Bible is still the traditional gift for a person entering ministry or graduating high school.

Things are different now. With Bible Gateway or YouVersion's Bible App, everyone with internet has free access to dozens of Bible translations, and can switch from one to another with the flick of a finger or the click of a mouse. I teach, preach, and do my personal Bible reading on my tablet, study on my phone, tablet, or laptop, and basically only open a paper Bible to get the page number for teaching notes.

But first, let's change the question. It's not really, which Bible should I read? There is only one Bible, which consists of the books that the Church established as official hundreds of years ago.[179] It was written in three languages: Hebrew (the overwhelming majority of the Old Testament), Aramaic (a few portions in the Old Testament), and one specific form of Ancient Greek[180] (the entire New Testament). The real question is, which translation should I use?

The good news, as I mentioned, is that there are literally dozens of English translations available. The bad news is,

---

[179] I cover this in the main part of the book.

[180] *Koine* Greek, if you want the exact name. And being able to translate a language (as some of us learned to do with *Koine* Greek) is a long way from reading for understanding and being able to think in the language. And in case you're curious, modern Greek is almost a completely different language.

well, there are literally dozens of English translations. So, the key questions are, what's the deal with all these translations, and how do I pick which one I should be reading for my own personal growth?

And now, because you didn't pick up a book called *Faith: In Your Own Handwriting* so the author could tell you everything to think, we'll dig into some serious stuff. Translation theory. This could get a little hairy, but stick with me. It's only a few paragraphs.

Translation theory concerns determining the best method to translate the Bible from its original languages into the language we all speak. On the surface, that doesn't sound difficult. Every time we see the Greek word for horse, we write "horse." Unfortunately, it isn't even remotely that simple.

Different languages don't just use different words. They have different sets of language rules.

For instance, English is a word-order language. A standard English sentence can be broken down into the subject, which will be near the front of the sentence, followed by the verb, which is frequently followed by a direct object. The most basic English sentence is, "The subject verbed the object." We know which noun is doing the action and which is being acted on by where they are located in the sentence. After we've got the subject-verb-object skeleton in place, we then sprinkle in a few adjectives, adverbs and prepositional phrases to spice things up.

Greek doesn't work that way. You can pretty much put the words in any order you want. Word order doesn't determines function, word form does. To oversimplify, if a noun is the subject, you add one set of letters to the end. If it's the object you use different last letters. A noun used in a prepositional phrase utilizes a different ending. In a similar way, verbs change their form based on lots of criteria, including whether their subject is male or female, singular or plural, or what tense they are. English does a little of this, but to nowhere near the extent Greek does.

Instead of driving function, word order is used for style and emphasis. If the author wants to stress the verb, they can make the verb the first word in the sentence. Or the last word. In the Greek, the word order for *"God so loved the world..."* is *"So for loved God the world..."* Just taking each Greek word and subbing in its English equivalent leaves us with a garbled mess, so word-substitution is not a valid translation theory.

Additionally, words don't always mean the same thing even within a language. When I say trunk, am I talking about the base of a tree, the back storage section of a car, a box in my attic, or an elephant's nose? Sometimes a trunk is where I store my spare tire, and sometimes it's how a peanut is transported into an elephant's mouth. Choosing the right word in the target language is crucial if I want to accurately convey an author's meaning.

And then there are idioms, metaphors, similes, and other intriguing uses of words. In English, you can "go to the bathroom" without going into a room. In Hebrew there is an idiom involving "one who pees against a wall," which is simply a colorful (and somewhat disgusting) way of saying "a dude."[181] If I'm translating that into English, should I discuss urination, just say "man," or find something in between these two extremes?[182]

These challenges lead to two primary theories of how to translate from the Biblical languages into modern English. One approach is to try to be as literal as possible. Strive to maintain the word order of the original as much as possible, and always try to translate each specific Greek or Hebrew word with the same English word.

We've already seen why absolute literal translation is impossible. Trying to maintain the word order of John 3:16 produces more confusion than insight. Determining which

---

[181] 1 Samuel 25:22, 34, among others.
[182] The King James Version took the colorful option, while every other translation I checked went with some variation of "males."

specific meaning of a word the author intended is crucial if you don't want to be looking for your spare tire in an elephant's nose. And am I helping people understand what is being said in 1 Samuel if they have to figure out what the heck peeing against a wall implies?

The second theory is called Dynamic Equivalence. This method tries to translate thought-for-thought instead of word-for-word. It turns "So for loved God the world…" into "This is how much God loved the world."[183] Works great sometimes. But not always.

Frequently, as the writers of the Bible were "carried along by the Holy Spirit,"[184] God inspired very specific words that carry very specific meanings. When John 3:16 says, "God so loved the world," is it significant that the Greek word behind "world" is *cosmos* (the entire created universe), whereas when Jesus tells His followers to take the Good News throughout the world, He uses *ethnos*, which means "nations."?[185] I tend to think so.

So, which theory is best, word-for-word or thought-for-thought? It's pretty obvious the answer is both, and every translation has to use both techniques sometimes. However, every translation tends toward one end or the other. *The Message* (MSG)[186] wedges itself firmly on the thought-for-thought end, while the *English Standard Version* (ESV) leans heavily toward the word-for-word, literal end. The *New International Version* (NIV) tries to find a sweet spot in the middle.

Other prominent translations that lean toward word-for-word include the *New American Standard* (NASB), the *Holman Christian Standard Bible* (HCSB), and the *King James Version* (KJV). Meanwhile, the *Contemporary English Version* (CEV), *New Century Version* (NCV), and *God's Word Translation*

---

[183] John 3:16 (MSG)

[184] 2 Peter 1:21 (NIV)

[185] Matthew 28:19

[186] For convenience, all the translations have three- or four-letter abbreviations.

(GW)[187] lean more toward thought-for-thought.

Which should you use? That's a personal decision. Feel free to experiment.

If you're drawn toward a literal translation, love poetic phrasing, and are comfortable with Shakespearean English, the *King James Version* could be for you. Or, if you can't fully get the hang of the older word forms, you could try the *New King James* (NKJV).

If you're new to the whole Christian thing, *The Message* could be a good place to start. I grew up reading *The Living Bible* (TLB), which *The Message* has basically replaced, and I think that's one reason the Bible stories always seem so alive to me.

Otherwise, experiment. Pick one of the ones I mentioned and read it for a few weeks to see how it helps you understand things.

Then, pick another and give it a test drive. I regularly read from two or three,[188] balancing both translation theories, to get as full an understanding of a passage as I can. Thankfully, while reading and comparing multiple translations used to be a major challenge, with our technology today, it's as simple as a flick of the fingers.

A Biblical language scholar wrote that, with all the translations we have available today, simply comparing multiple translations can give you a better picture of what the original author was trying to convey than learning the original languages for yourself.

Pick two or three translations and take advantage of this privilege.

---

[187] They didn't get the abbreviation memo.
[188] I primarily utilize the NIV, NLT, and ESV.

END TIMES:
FOUR PROMINENT VIEWS,
AND WHAT JESUS' FIRST COMING
SHOULD TEACH US ABOUT HIS SECOND

When it comes to the specifics of the Second Coming, there are four main viewpoints. Each has strong support from very smart people of God. These disagreements center on how to interpret a handful of major themes the Bible teaches about Jesus' return.

Tribulation. Just like it sounds, this is not a pleasant time. In a sense, it's sort of God's Pre-judgment.

Millennium. The flip side of Tribulation, this is a time when God is large and in charge. Things are going His way.

Rapture of Believers. Remember that passage about all of us being changed? This is when that happens.

Jesus' Physical Return. Not hard to understand. Jesus rides in on the clouds and fixes (or starts fixing) everything.

The basic concepts aren't too difficult, and all seem to be clearly taught in the Bible. But how do they work together to finish history? That's where the complications come in. Basically, there are four principle theories for integrating these events. I would say that the four have been prominent for most of church history, but one of them was rather late to the party. (You can decide whether that's a point for or against it.)

Dispensational Premillennialism

If you've read the *Left Behind* books, this is the theory found in those books. In Dispensational Premillennialism, the Tribulation is a literal seven-year period of really, really bad things. The Rapture of Christians happens at the very beginning of the Tribulation.[189] At the end of the seven years,

---

[189] There are a significant number of Dispensational Premillennialist who believe in what is known as a mid-tribulation Rapture, meaning that the Church gets taken

Jesus returns and sets up a thousand-year Millennium Kingdom. At the end of the thousand years, there is a final defeat of Satan and eternity truly begins.

This view is very popular now, but it is the new kid on the block when it comes to eschatology (fancy word for the study of end times). It is also the only view of the four that separates the Rapture and the Return. Many present-day popular authors and pastors teach this view.

Historical Premillennialism

This isn't much different from Dispensational Premillennialism except that in the prior view the Church gets to skip all or most of the Tribulation. In Historical Premillennialism the Church endures the Tribulation before Jesus returns, raptures the Church and begins his Millennial Kingdom. In this view, the Tribulation may or may not be exactly seven years.

This view has been widespread throughout Church history, and remains popular today. Prominent early church leaders like Irenaeus and Justin Martyr held this view, and a recent survey found that a slim majority of the Southern Baptist seminary professors support it as well.

Postmillennialism

This is the most optimistic view. This theory holds that the world has been going through Tribulation since Jesus. However, the Christian impact on the world will gradually increase, and the societies of the world will gradually improve as General Tribulation gives way to a Millennial Reign of the Church. Jesus returns at the end, and establishes His Eternal Kingdom.

This view was very popular among the revivalist preachers

---

out half-way through the Tribulation. Other than that variation, they fit into this theory, and I didn't want to bog down the discussion trying to differentiate the two.

of the 1700-1800's, including Jonathan Edwards, B.B. Warfield, and Charles Hodge. Just like the general optimism in the West that was flattened by World War I, Postmillennialism has struggled since then. However, prominent pastor and theologian R.C. Sproul holds this view today.

Realized Millennialism

In this view (also known as amillennialism) Jesus' Millennial Reign began at Pentecost and will continue until His Return and the Rapture of the Church. Tribulation will increase significantly as His return grows closer.

Like Historical Premillennialism, this view has been prominent throughout Church history, from Augustine of Hippo (fourth century), to Protestant reformers like John Calvin, and many theologians today. This is also the official view of the Roman Catholic Church.

If you want to dig more deeply into this, *Four Views of the End Times* by Timothy Paul Jones in excellent booklet that provides a balanced perspective. If you want to research any single view, well, the options seem limitless.

What Jesus' First Coming Should Teach Us about His Second

As the name implies, we are waiting for Jesus' *Second* Coming. Well, did you ever notice that when Jesus came the first time, no one was expecting Him, even though a) every Jew was hoping for Messiah to come soon, and b) they knew the Old Testament and its prophecies even better than we do? (It wouldn't be uncommon for a rabbi to have the whole Old Testament memorized, and almost all would have memorized the first five books.)

Which should lead to a simple question: Why were they so surprised?

In trying to answer that question, I realized that Jesus'

First Coming fulfilled four different types of prophecies.

The first were **Clear Prophecies**. Micah 5:2 is one of these. It says the Messiah will come from Bethlehem. The scholars of Jesus' day got this one right.[190] They expected the Messiah to be born in Bethlehem.

It gets more complicated from there, because the next type are **Hidden Prophecies**. Psalm 22 is an amazing example. If you read the New Testament accounts of Jesus' crucifixion, then read Psalm 22, you will see that it describes the event in amazing detail. And it was written 500 or so years ahead of time.

But here's the thing. Up until Jesus quoted the first line of it from the cross, no one knew it was about Him. And there were lots of hidden prophecies, verses that talked about Jesus' First Coming without giving clear evidence in advance to help readers understand that they were prophetic.

Then we come to the **Picture Prophecies**, stories like Genesis 22 where Abraham is called to sacrifice his own son. (God stops him at the last second.) No Christian can read that story without seeing that it pictures God sending His own Son to die for us. And when God stops Abraham, and we remember that Abraham had already said, "*God will provide a lamb,*" we can't help but be reminded that Jesus was "the Lamb of God who takes away the sin of the world."[191]

It's an amazing prophetic image, but once again, there are no clues in this or any other of these Old Testament pictures that let readers know ahead of time that they were prophecies.

And if you thought those were challenging, we'll now look at **Dual-Fulfillment Prophecies**. These are predictions in the Old Testament that had already been fulfilled before Jesus came, and were then "re-fulfilled" in a deeper way by Jesus.

A great example of this is Isaiah 7. "*The Lord himself will give you a sign: The virgin will be with child and will give birth to a son, and*

---

[190] Matthew 2:3-6
[191] John 1:29

will call him Immanuel."[192] Super prediction about the Virgin Birth.

But here's the thing. The prophecy in Isaiah 7 had already been fulfilled once, not in the sense of a literal virgin giving birth, but in the sense of a young maiden going through the normal process, as you can see if you read all of Isaiah 7:10-16.

> *Therefore the Lord himself will give you a sign: The virgin will conceive and give birth to a son, and will call him Immanuel. He will be eating curds and honey when he knows enough to reject the wrong and choose the right, for before the boy knows enough to reject the wrong and choose the right, the land of the two kings you dread will be laid waste.*[193]

The prophecy specifically mentions the land of two kings[194] being laid waste, and the nation of Assyria invading instead (verse 17). All of this took place well before Jesus. Matter of fact, it happened within the time frame Isaiah mentions, the time necessary for a young woman to conceive, give birth to, and begin raising a child.

Matthew reapplied this prophecy and clearly taught that Mary was a virgin when Jesus was born. But let's say there was a scholar living prior to Jesus' birth who compiled a list of all the prophecies found in the Old Testament. After finishing the list, he then split the list into prophecies that had already been fulfilled and those that had yet to be fulfilled. On which list would he have put this prophecy?

Yep, on the "fulfilled" list. And there is basically no way to tell from the prophecy itself that it was also talking about Jesus and Mary.

There are many, many more prophecies that fit into the "less-clear" categories. Jesus even spent much of His time after the Resurrection showing to His followers all the

---

[192] Isaiah 7:14 (ESV)

[193] Isaiah 7:14-16 (NIV)

[194] The Kingdom of Aram and the Northern Kingdom of Israel

passages from the Old Testament they didn't know were about Him.[195]

Which leaves us with four types of prophecy and a huge question. If Jesus' Second Coming is like His first, how can we be confident that we have identified all the Clear Prophecies, Hidden Prophecies, Picture Prophecies, and Dual-Fulfillment Prophecies necessary to get everything right?

That question should lead us back to a closer examination of what Jesus actually said about His return, and the primary purpose of prophecy.

What Jesus Said about His Second Coming

Jesus had risen from the dead, and His disciples had lots of questions. Just before He went back to the Father, they asked one of their most pressing: *"Lord, are you at this time going to restore the kingdom to Israel?"* [196]

Are you going to restore the Kingdom now, and if not, when? In other words, teach us about the end times.

Jesus' response is telling. We'll look at it in two sections. First, the direct answer: *"It is not for you to know the times or dates the Father has set by his own authority.* [197]

Now, correct me if I'm wrong, but it sounds like they asked when He was coming back, and He politely said, "It's none of your business."

And if you think that was pointed, look at the second part of His answer:

"But you will receive power when the Holy Spirit comes on you; and you will be my witnesses in Jerusalem, and in all Judea and Samaria, and to the ends of the earth." [198]

So, to put the whole thing together, the disciples asked Jesus to tell them the details about the end times. Jesus

---

[195] Luke 24:25-27
[196] Acts 1:6 (NIV)
[197] Acts 1:7 (NIV)
[198] Acts 1:8 (NIV)

replied, "That's none of your business. Instead of worrying about that, get to work telling people about me, which, by the way, is your business."

Which fits very neatly into why God gives us prophecy in the Bible to begin with (and it's probably not what you think).

The Purpose of Prophecy

A lot of people seem to think that God put prophecy in the Bible to tell us the future. But He didn't. See, God's just not that into giving people facts. If He was we might know how tall Jesus was, whether He was left or right handed, and which Tuesday in June Jesus is returning. But we don't.

Obviously, God has other purposes in mind than giving us information so we can pass some sort of Bible trivia test.

So what is God looking for when He speaks?

Well, in the verses we just looked at, He wants us to spread the good news about Jesus. (The word Gospel, by the way, means "good news.") The Old Testament prophetic book of Micah talks about how God isn't that crazy about sacrifices, then says:

What does the LORD require of you? To act justly and to love mercy and to walk humbly with your God.[199]

And in the New Testament book of James, we're told:

"Pure and genuine religion in the sight of God the Father means caring for orphans and widows in their distress and refusing to let the world corrupt you."[200]

Throughout the Bible, God's desire is to draw us closer to Himself in relationship, and to change our attitudes and actions. This is especially true in the prophetic books (everything from Isaiah to the last book in the Old Testament, Malachi). God's desire is to get people to live into His will. That is the primary purpose of prophecy.

[199] Micah 6:8 (NIV)
[200] James 1:27 (NLT)

The Book of Jonah is an excellent example. Jonah, the racist prophet,[201] is sent to Nineveh. There he preaches to a people whom he doesn't like, gleefully telling them that God is going to annihilate them. He's obviously predicting the future. But the thing is, even though it annoys Jonah, the people of Nineveh accept his teaching, reform their behavior, and turn to God. Because God's goal for Jonah's prophecy wasn't the destruction of Nineveh, but rather the restoration of these people to Himself, God doesn't destroy Nineveh,[202] much to Jonah's disappointment.

Prophecy had two components: foretelling, predicting the future, and "forth-telling", instructing the listeners to change their ways. And the foretelling was always just a tool for the forth-telling. So, when Jesus and the rest of the New Testament tell us that Jesus is coming, the point isn't to get us to draw up charts and hold End-time conferences. The point is for us to get busy doing the things He told us to do, like telling others about Jesus, and living out God's principles of love, mercy, and justice.

---

[201] Seriously. Not a prophet to promote racism, but rather a racist who God used pretty much against his will.

[202] Yet. Their revival isn't permanent, and they do eventually face a judgment of literally Biblical proportions.

ADDITIONAL RESOURCES

Here is a list of books to help you dig more deeply into an area discussed in the book. Of course, there are dozens of great books in each area, but these are good places to start. (Some of the books span multiple categories but are only listed in one.)

Apologetics: the logical, scientific, and historical defense of the faith.
On Guard: Defending Your Faith with Reason and Precision, William Lane Craig.
The Case for Christ: A Journalist's Personal Investigation of the Evidence of Jesus, Lee Strobel
The Case for Faith: A Journalist Investigates the Toughest Objections to Christianity, Lee Strobel
The Reason for God: Belief in an Age of Skepticism, Timothy Keller

General Theology
Mere Christianity, C.S. Lewis
Knowing God, J.I.Packer...

Prayer, Bible Reading, and Other Habits of Faith
Prayer: Experiencing Awe and Intimacy with God, Timothy Keller
The Circle Maker: Praying Circles Around Your Biggest Dreams and Greatest Fears, Mark Batterson
How to Read the Bible for All It's Worth, Gordon D. Fee and Douglas Stuart
How to Read the Bible Book by Book: A Guided Tour, Gordon D. Fee, and Douglas Stuart

The Complete Idiot's Guide to the Bible, James Stuart Bell, Jr., and Stan Campbell
Celebration of Discipline, Richard Foster

Commitment
In a Pit with a Lion on a Snowy Day, Mark Batterson
Crazy Love: Overwhelmed by a Relentless God, Francis Chan
Interrupted: When Jesus Wrecks Your Comfortable Christianity, Jen Hatmaker

Trials and Temptations
The Screwtape Letters, C.S. Lewis
Margin: Restoring Emotional, Physical, Financial, and Time Reserves to Overloaded Lives, Richard Swenson

Other Great Books to Help You Write Your Faith
What's So Amazing about Grace, Philip Yancey (Okay, any book by Philip Yancey)
The Ragamuffin Gospel: Good News for the Bedraggled, Beat-Up, and Burnt Out, Brennan Manning
My Utmost for His Highest, Oswald Chambers (Daily Readings)
The Pursuit of God, A.W. Tozer

ABOUT THE AUTHOR

Steve Davis is the Lead and Founding Pastor of Spout Springs
Church near Fayetteville, NC. He and his wife Kim have three
daughters, Nikki, Sierra, and Dominique, and one grandson, TJ. He
was ordained in1986, and has been in full-time ministry since 1996.
He has published two other books: *Evolving: My Journey to Reconcile
Science and Faith*, and *Transform(180)*. In his spare time he talks
incessantly about CrossFit.

26648848R00086

Made in the USA
San Bernardino, CA
02 December 2015